LEARNING OBJECTIVES FOR:

PROBLEM SOLVING FOR TEAMS

The objectives for *Problem Solving Solving for Teams* are listed below. They have been developed to guide you the user to the core issues covered in this book.

THE OBJECTIVES OF THIS BOOK ARE TO HELP THE USER:

1) Learn problem-solving techniques that work

2) Understand how to define a problem

3) Master skills in problem analysis

4) Learn tools for decision making

5) Explore ways to implement decision making

ASSESSING PROGRESS

A Crisp Series **assessment** is available for this book. The 25-item, multiple-choice and true/false questionnaire allows the reader to evaluate his or her comprehension of the subject matter.

To download the assessment and answer key, go to www.axzopress.com and search on the book title.

Assessments should not be used in any employee selection process.

ABOUT THE AUTHOR

Sandy Pokras is president of Viability Group Inc., a team-building, communication training and management consulting firm in Northern California. He has been active in management training and consulting since 1973 and holds a certificate in Interpersonal Counseling from the Advance Organization of Copenhagen. His training workshops teach team managers, leaders, facilitators and members to achieve high-performance teamwork.

As a corporate consultant, program designer, keynote speaker, and conference facilitator, Mr. Pokras conducts sessions for a wide range of organizations, including IBM, Chevron, the Federal Reserve Bank, Westinghouse, Siemens, the University of California and the U.S. Postal Service.

Mr. Pokras is the author of numerous management articles as well as *Rapid Team Deployment* and *Working in Teams*, published by Crisp Publications in 1995 and 1997, respectively.

Problem Solving for Teams

A Systematic Approach to Consensus Decision Making

Revised Edition

Sandy Pokras

A Crisp Fifty-Minute™ *Series Book*

This Fifty-Minute™ book is designed to be "read with a pencil." It is an excellent workbook for self-study as well as classroom learning. All material is copyright-protected and cannot be duplicated without permission from the publisher. *Therefore, be sure to order a copy for every training participant through our Web site, www.axzopress.com.*

Problem Solving for Teams

A Systematic Approach to Consensus Decision Making

Revised Edition

Sandy Pokras

The message from the moon ... is that no problem need be considered insolvable.

–Norman Cousins

CREDITS:

VP, Product Development: **Charlie Blum**
Editors: **Michael G. Crisp and Francine Lundy Ruvolo**
Production Editor: **Genevieve McDermott**
Production Artists: **Nicole Phillips, Rich Lehl, and Betty Hopkins**

Trademarks
Crisp Fifty-Minute Series is a trademark of Axzo Press.

Some of the product names and company names used in this book have been used for identification purposes only and may be trademarks or registered trademarks of their respective manufacturers and sellers.

Disclaimer
We reserve the right to revise this publication and make changes from time to time in its content without notice.

ISBN 10: 1-4188-8913-X
ISBN 13: 978-1-4188-8913-5
Library of Congress Catalog Card Number 94-72611
Printed in the United States of America

4 5 6 7 12 11 100

CONTENTS

CONTENTS (continued)

INTRODUCTION

Have you heard the old cliché *"There are no problems, only opportunities"*? This might sound like pie-in-the-sky optimism to anyone stuck in the middle of a difficult puzzle or a stressful people problem. But by using the proven, logical problem-solving and decision-making system presented in this book you can create opportunities from problems.

This book will show your team how to rationally confront problems and systematically resolve crises. The decision-making methods you learn will help you break down touchy situations into component parts which can easily be dealt with individually. By using the comprehensive system presented, you'll know how to define, unravel, analyze and solve tough dilemmas and recurring foul-ups.

Throughout this book, when you see the word team we simply mean...

A group of willing and trained individuals who are united around a common goal.

We could be talking about:

- a natural work group
- an ad hoc meeting of concerned employees
- a management team
- a cross-functional council
- a quality improvement team

In the best of cases, teams that have the best success solving problems are structured to work together, share responsibility for their task, depend on each other in some way, and are empowered to implement consensus decisions.

PART I
PROBLEM SOLVING AND DECISION MAKING

THE BENEFITS AND SKILLS

By following the steps of systematic problem solving and decision making you and your team can prevent problems from recurring. The steps include . . .

STEP 1: **PROBLEM RECOGNITION**
STEP 2: **PROBLEM LABELING**
STEP 3: **PROBLEM-CAUSE ANALYSIS**
STEP 4: **OPTIONAL SOLUTIONS**
STEP 5: **DECISION MAKING**
STEP 6: **IMPLEMENTATION**

Those who apply the techniques of *Team Problem Solving* will receive the following benefits and learn the following skills:

- Definitions   You and your team will learn to accurately define the real problem to avoid solving symptoms.

- Solutions   You and your team can implement once-and-for-all solutions instead of temporary ''band-aid'' fixes.

- Decisions   The decisions you and your team make will be good decisions that can be implemented and will stick.

- Meetings   Your team meetings will reflect productive problem solving and decision making.

- Buy-in   You and your team will learn to obtain buy-in from conflicting viewpoints to help define problems, reach decisions, clarify solutions and implement action plans.

- Teamwork   You will enjoy effective teamwork between differing individuals and groups while solving problems.

EXPECTATIONS WORKSHEET

Write your answers below:

What problem situations would your team like to correct?

What difficult decisions does your team need to work through logically?

Which recurring problems and decisions would your team like to resolve once-and-for-all?

What problem-solving and decision-making skills does your team need to improve?

Select one of the above answers to use as your Team Case Problem, to systematically solve, while working through this book.

As you work through this book, refer back to this worksheet. Experience has shown that this is the best way to learn a self-development method like this.

TEAM LEARNING OBJECTIVES

Rate your interest in the following objectives.

OBJECTIVES RATING — We want to:	Top Priority	Interested	Some Interest	Little Interest
1) Understand the *steps* of this problem-solving system.	☐	☐	☐	☐
2) Know how to use the analytical *tools* in each step.	☐	☐	☐	☐
3) Recognize the vital role *communication* plays at each step.	☐	☐	☐	☐
4) Know what *questions* to use in order to stimulate communication at each step.	☐	☐	☐	☐
5) Understand the *anatomy* of problems and why they persist.	☐	☐	☐	☐
6) Understand how to confront problems to *prevent future stress.*	☐	☐	☐	☐
7) Know how to distinguish between the *causes and effects* of problems.	☐	☐	☐	☐
8) Know how to *label* a problem to facilitate discussion and analysis.	☐	☐	☐	☐
9) Know how to find a problem's *root cause.*	☐	☐	☐	☐
10) Know how to brainstorm optional *solutions.*	☐	☐	☐	☐
11) Know how to evaluate optional solutions to *decide* on the most workable strategy.	☐	☐	☐	☐
12) Understand the importance of action planning to *implement* the chosen solution.	☐	☐	☐	☐
13) Know how to *apply* the system to real-life problems as they occur.	☐	☐	☐	☐

TEAM COMMITMENT

You and your team have had a chance to clarify your expectations and objectives. Your next step is to make an active commitment. The *Team Learning Contract* below presents the essential items. Check each item to which you will commit. Then sign your name as an affirmation of your commitment. If you are working this book together, each team member should sign their name as well.

TEAM LEARNING CONTRACT

Check
Your
Commitment

The team plans to be more logical, analytical and systematic in solving problems and making decisions. _____

The team wants to take steps to ensure we find the "real problem" before beginning to solve it. _____

The team is willing to involve others affected by the problem in the solution process in order to promote support and teamwork. _____

The team is willing to work through the exercises in this book, do our best to relate them to the problem to be solved and then implement our solutions. _____

The team will manage time so we can concentrate on learning the skills presented in this book by studying them without distraction or interruption. _____

The team intends to use what is learned and consciously put it into practice. _____

Agreement:
The team wants to receive the maximum benefit from this program by carrying out this learning contract.

_____   _____
(signature)   (date)

PART II

PROCESS OVERVIEW

WHAT IS A PROBLEM ANYWAY?

What does the word *problem* mean? Since it is used so often in this book, you need a crystal-clear understanding of the word. What do you think "problem" means? Write your immediate thoughts below:

_____

_____

_____

_____

PROBLEM ANATOMY

A problem is basically a dilemma with no apparent way out; an undesirable situation without a solution; or a question that you can't currently answer. It's not just that things are different from the way you'd ideally like them to be—it's that you can't fix them no matter what you do.

The anatomy of a problem boils down to this simple picture:

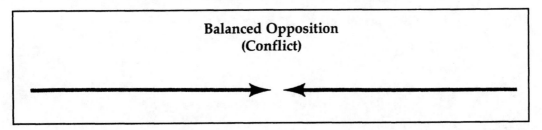

**Balanced Opposition
(Conflict)**

In words, a problem is an idea, force or goal opposed by a counter idea, force or goal. For example:

You want to go shopping	but	**you also want to save money.**
You have to work with J.R.	but	**you can't stand the person.**
Your department thinks everything is working fine	but	**your quality inspector wants some changes.**

The balanced opposition of situations is what generates stress and confusion. The balance makes the problem persist. If one side gets stronger and wins the struggle, the problem disappears. For example, your boss comes into the picture and decides how to handle things and everyone goes along with the decision.

PROBLEM ANATOMY QUIZ

Let's check your understanding of problem anatomy with the following quiz.

DIRECTIONS

Check the items below which are stated as problems:

- ☐ A question the team hasn't yet tried to answer.
- ☐ A question the team can't find an answer to.
- ☐ Your boss gives you a long project appropriate for your work.
- ☐ Your supervisor assigns a task the team doesn't have time to do.
- ☐ Should you reorganize the team's work area?
- ☐ More work than the team can finish before vacation season.
- ☐ A group goal that you can't achieve no matter what you try.
- ☐ You can't improve a process due to coworker resistance.
- ☐ You see several big opportunities for quality improvement.
- ☐ Should the team fight the system or just go along for the ride?

ANSWERS

1. no 2. yes 3. no 4. yes 5. no 6. yes 7. yes 8. yes 9. no 10. yes

PROBLEM CHARACTERISTICS

The following checklist summarizes the characteristics of problems. Items on this list always seem to be true about problems. It might be said that if these items exist, then your situation qualifies as a true problem. Check which of these characteristics apply to the cases you identified on the *Expectations Worksheet* on page 4.

Problem Characteristics Checklist

Characteristics	These apply to our situation
Incomplete communication: Conversations have broken down or haven't even been started so that full understanding is lacking.	☐
Unknowns: Information is missing.	☐
Inaccurate information: Some of the known information is wrong.	☐
Confusion: People involved find themselves in a mental fog, stressed or overwhelmed by stimuli and choices.	☐
Hidden emotions: Emerging feelings tend to come out as you examine the situation.	☐
Different viewpoints: You and others have conflicting ideas.	☐
Changing impressions: As you investigate the situation, ideas, feelings and explanations change, sometimes radically.	☐
Balanced dilemma: A tug of war exists where no one person or idea is able to win.	☐
Persistence: The situation won't disappear.	☐

CONSUMER TECH CASE PROBLEM

To make the techniques presented in this book more realistic, consider the situation in the *Consumer Tech Case Problem.* Throughout the book we will apply the methods presented to this problem.

Consumer Tech Case Problem

Consumer Tech is a small company which develops and sells consumer products based on new technology. They have an extremely successful product, the Automatic Toothbrush. Recently, the Engineering Department came up with a dramatic new improvement. They've perfected a hands-free circuit which allows the brush to clean teeth electronically. Its called the Electronic Toothbrush.

This has created a problem: The Engineering Manager wants to introduce the development right away. Unfortunately, during test production runs, the Manufacturing Manager has encountered problems producing the new components. The Quality Manager is helping to determine what's causing the problems.

The Marketing Manager wants to announce the improvements immediately, but the Finance Manager is worried about making the large inventory of Automatic Toothbrushes obsolete if the introduction is done too quickly.

Formal meetings about the Electronic Toothbrush, led by the company President, quickly deteriorate into heated arguments which lead nowhere, and impromptu water-cooler meetings in the hall often become shouting matches.

Looking at the *Problem Characteristics Checklist* on page 11, you will find all the problem characteristics present in this situation. Consumer Tech has tried to find a solution but things are not progressing. It's becoming increasingly clear that some balanced opposition that no one has yet recognized needs immediate attention. Unless this conflict is uncovered and resolved, things will probably go from bad to worse.

CONSUMER TECH PROBLEM—
YOUR TEAM'S RESPONSE

If you wanted to help, what would you do? Write your thoughts below. Feel free to refer to anything you have read thus far in this book. Later, after you have completed the book, revisit this page to see how your suggestions have changed.

The team would help Consumer Tech by:

PROBLEM-SOLVING METHODOLOGY

The ideal method of resolving problems and making difficult decisions involves two steps. This magic formula is guaranteed to work. In fact, it's never failed when applied correctly. Here it is:

I. Define the problem.

II. Decide how to solve it.

You already knew that, right? Although it seems obvious, most problem solvers and decision makers don't do a very good job of Phase I, Problem Recognition. Instead, they rush off to Phase II, Solution Decision. Unless you define the problem thoroughly and accurately, your solution may not address what's really wrong underneath. In fact, most students of this system report that finding solutions is relatively easy. The difficulty is knowing exactly what to analyze and resolve.

How do you define a problem? And how do you find the best solution? Take a look at the *Problem-Solving/Decision-Making Outline* presented on page 15. This summarizes the process, and will be referred to as the PS/DM Outline throughout the book. Let's see how it works.

"BEFORE I STATE THE PROBLEM, ARE THERE ANY SOLUTIONS?"

PROBLEM-SOLVING/ DECISION-MAKING OUTLINE

Each step of the following outline has a specific result. Only when you reach that result should you go on to the next step. For the best results don't skip *any* step.

PROBLEM-DEFINITION PROCESS	RESULT
1. Recognition Discuss and document individual views, proven facts and relevant symptoms, until everyone involved accepts that there is a problem.	**Agreement that an issue needs resolution.**
2. Label Clearly document all sides of the exact conflict you want to resolve.	**An agreed-upon statement of the problem.**
3. Analysis Find and agree on the *single* most fundamental source of the problem.	**Unanimous identification of the root cause which needs correcting.**

SOLUTION DECISION-MAKING PROCESS	RESULT
4. Options List *all* alternative solutions that have the slightest chance of resolving the problem and its root cause.	**A complete list of possible solutions.**
5. Decision Making Choose the best solution on your list by objectively evaluating the optional strategies.	**A firm joint decision on the chosen solution.**
6. Implementation Organize tasks, timing, people and resources into a step-by-step action plan, implement it and then standardize the process.	**The solution is translated into a permanent new reality.**

Each step of this outline will be discussed in detail throughout the balance of this book. Before going into each step in detail, consider the example and overview checklist that follow.

SAMPLE PROBLEM-SOLVING/ DECISION-MAKING OUTLINE

Here's an actual example of how the PS/DM outline was used to solve a team problem...

PROBLEM DEFINTION
1. Recognition Trouble with new 24-hour monitored alarm system. Frustrating, doesn't do everything promised. Terrible service, don't show for appointments.
2. Label Can't hear tripped alarm in work area as demonstrated by sales representative.
3. Analysis Poor service so customer problems don't get fixed. Too big, busy and disorganized. Communication breakdown between phone service reps, technicians and maintenance supervisor. Demonstrated last year's model with internal alarm.
Root Cause: The new model installed doesn't have the internal alarm capability demonstrated by the sales representative.

SOLUTION DECISION
4. Options Refuse to pay bill. Go to court Replace alarm system. Add an inside horn to the existing system. Use the alarm system the way it is and hope for the best.
5. Decision Making Add an inside horn to the existing system.
6. Implementation The maintenance supervisor personally installed the inside horn, consulting with the team to make sure it was acceptable. There was no charge for service or labor, but we paid for the extra horn. (If we hadn't we would have alienated the management of the security service hired to protect us.)

OVERVIEW CHECKLIST

Review the checklist below to evaluate how well you currently deal with problems and decisions. You can refer back to it whenever you want to check your status.

> Check those things you do currently when making a decision or solving a problem:

We plan an agenda directed to a specific result. ☐

We stay on track and follow the planned agenda. ☐

We set and stick to ground rules for participation. ☐

We break down big problems into "bite-sized" chunks. ☐

We complete each step before moving to the next. ☐

We return to the previous step if progress bogs down. ☐

We know which technique to use at each point. ☐

We trust the process and keep on it as long as it works. ☐

We don't mix methods from different processes. ☐

We include all people or units affected. ☐

We openly consider divergent ideas as valuable input. ☐

We accept and integrate all views and feelings. ☐

We write down all thoughts, suggestions and input. ☐

We keep a public running record of team discussion. ☐

We keep all material visible to all team members. ☐

We know which questions to ask at each step. ☐

We draw out complete answers from all present. ☐

We discipline ourselves to listen and respond. ☐

We assign distinct roles in the meeting. ☐

We stimulate the team synergy and creativity. ☐

We seek agreement between divergent positions. ☐

PART III

COMMUNICATION DYNAMICS

COMMUNICATION DYNAMICS

Before starting the six-step process outlined on page 15, do you know what determines whether or not a problem solving or decision-making team can make the process work? If you answered communication skills, you are right.

Poor communication causes barriers to solutions, while good communication skills are strong catalysts to problem solving. Poor communication is an indication of the existence of a problem and may, in fact, be the cause.

This part presents some critical mechanics to make communication work during the problem-solving and decision-making process.

REACHING AGREEMENT

Without mutual agreement that a problem exists, it can't be discussed, analyzed or solved effectively. Good problem solvers and decision makers achieve agreement by applying this vital awareness. Communication is the process to make all this work.

The information on the following page summarizes *Guidelines* for making the logical process work with human beings who sometimes are not so logical. *How To Apply It* defines how to implement each guideline.

HOW TO GET AGREEMENT ON PROBLEMS

GUIDELINE	HOW TO APPLY IT
If one team member feels there is a problem with someone or something, then there **definitely is** a problem.	Don't ignore it or let yourself be talked out of it. Probe for others' awareness of the problem.
If a problem exists, everyone is **aware** of it in some way. Remember that one teammate's **awareness** of a problem may be quite different from others.	To find out another's awareness of a problem, ask how things are different from the way they should be, or simply ask what their awareness of the problem is.
Find an accepted or observable fact as a **reference** point to start with.	Use production statistics, specific events, confirmed facts, something the other person has said, but no value judgments.
Find where **viewpoints** overlap.	Analyze the information you receive from everyone and see what's in common.
Ask before you dictate.	State the general area you want to talk about, but immediately ask for the other person's feelings, thoughts or observations.
Solicit other **points of view.**	Don't force your viewpoint on them, but show empathy for their position until they accept yours.
Avoid a **threatening** accusing climate.	Don't use leading or judgmental questions (*"Are you still screwing up?"*) or lectures that elicit guilt or impose value judgments.
Create a strong and open working **relationship.**	If you're confronted with severe defensiveness or intimidation, use a less threatening approach.
Discover the **unknowns** that are causing the problem to persist.	Keep communicating until you find them.

WHAT MAKES TEAM MEETINGS WORK?

Let's apply the guidelines from the previous page to team meetings. Think back to several recent group problem-solving or decision-making situations you were involved in. What made the meetings work and what got in the way?

To answer this question, use the following **Force-Field Analysis** *Worksheet: Positive/Negative Forces For Meetings.* You will find this format several times later in this book. Two columns are headed by opposing brainstorming questions, in this case dealing with meetings. The question on the left asks for positive forces and the question on the right asks for negative forces. By playing a plus against a minus, a team's thinking loosens up and differences stand out more clearly.

When you fill in this form, don't use general terms like *"communication"* but specific descriptions like *"Joe wasn't prepared"* and *"Geri knew what questions to ask."*

FORCE-FIELD ANALYSIS WORKSHEET:
POSITIVE/NEGATIVE FORCES FOR MEETINGS

What makes our meetings productive and effective?	What makes our meetings unproductive and ineffective?

TEAM MEETING ROLES

Experts find that team meetings work best when roles are well-defined. The *Team Meeting Roles* chart below explains how to separate responsibilities for meeting participants. The *Discussion Moderator* or traffic cop and the *Recorder* or public note-taker are neutral. All team members should contribute as a *Participant* and a *Presenter.*

The most significant factor, the *Authority Figure* of the group, must relinquish roles to team members. If the authority figure doesn't do this, contributors will hold back, edit what they say or challenge authority. An effective team meeting will produce an open climate, a free exchange and creative thinking without undue concern about the boss's reaction. This is hard to achieve but defining roles will help.

TEAM MEETING ROLES

Discussion Moderator

Directs the traffic of the discussion. Announces each topic and its time frame, calls for input, asks stimulating questions, balances participation, reminds wanderers of the issue and summarizes at the end. Remains neutral and doesn't pass judgment without permission from the team. Since bosses are expected to be decisive, making one the discussion moderator usually distorts a free and open exchange.

Recorder

Keeps an accurate, public, running record of what is said. Writes key words clearly on a flip chart or blackboard so that speakers feel they were heard correctly. Doesn't try to document everything but just gets the main points down.

Presenters

Presents outside information and major viewpoints in a systematic fashion. Articulates the position, gives supporting evidence, involves listeners, leads their thought process and responds to questions.

Participants

Speak their minds fully and clearly, listen intently and absorb what others have to say.

Authority Figure

Ideally, the authority figure should contribute as a participant and a presenter. Since this is difficult in practice, it is recommended that the authority figure only assume the role of "special participant," the one with the final say.

THE DISCUSSION MODERATOR

The most challenging role is that of *Discussion Moderator* who directs the participation, but doesn't evaluate what is said.

Controlling a dialogue has three phases: 1) starting—getting individual or group discussions going, 2) guiding—steering the dialogue once started, and 3) stopping—summarizing, wrapping up or getting people to stop when they've already finished. These subskills are detailed in the following *Discussion Moderator Skills Checklist.* Use this checklist to assess the effectiveness of a discussion moderator and to identify those subskills needing development.

DISCUSSION MODERATOR SKILLS CHECKLIST

Starting Skills

- [ ] Know the issues before beginning.
- [ ] Have easy reference notes and outlines available.
- [ ] Get attention and call people to order.
- [ ] Announce agenda items.
- [ ] State points and problems clearly.
- [ ] Establish realistic time frames.
- [ ] Ask questions to get the team thinking.
- [ ] Call all people by name.
- [ ] Draw people out, especially quiet ones.
- [ ] Notice and call on those with something to say.
- [ ] Introduce new viewpoints into an ongoing discussion.

Guiding Skills

- [ ] Listen carefully to all participants.
- [ ] Use silence effectively and wait out pauses.
- [ ] Read indicators and body language.
- [ ] Remain neutral to ensure acceptance of all ideas.
- [ ] Be sensitive and adjust to moods to keep things moving.
- [ ] Follow the agenda and keep discussions on track.
- [ ] Restate topic to focus the team on one issue at a time.
- [ ] Steer discussions toward the desired results.

THE DISCUSSION MODERATOR (continued)

Guiding Skills (continued)

☐ Clarify meanings and restate questions.

☐ Avoid interfering with interactions.

☐ Turn provocative questions back to the team for discussion.

☐ Balance participation between different styles.

☐ Mediate conflicting viewpoints so all are heard.

☐ Manage diversions, digressions and distractions.

☐ Watch the clock and keep time frames apparent.

☐ Reflect on repeating patterns and ask for reactions.

Stopping Skills

☐ Acknowledge what people have said.

☐ Ensure each participant gets to finish.

☐ Prevent individuals from talking at inappropriate times.

☐ Stop people who say things over and over.

☐ Protect individuals by discouraging attackers.

☐ Let long-winded dominators know they've been heard.

☐ Check that questioners receive satisfactory answers.

☐ Announce when time deadlines are approaching.

☐ Summarize what has been accomplished.

☐ Know when to recap by listening for common themes.

☐ Show consensus by noticing and announcing it.

☐ Ask for decisions and suggest conclusions.

DOCUMENTATION DURING TEAM MEETINGS

Effective problem-solving and decision-making teams keep accurate, up-to-date, legible notes. The real pay-off of good paperwork habits comes during later phases of the PS/DM Outline.

Because of the confusion factor, especially at the beginning of a problem-solving situation, all sorts of information will be mixed together. If you carefully document items as you go along, you'll come to a decision sooner than those who do a poor job of recording the process.

Benefits of Documentation

- Provides clearer, more accurate communication
- Formally acknowledges individual contributions
- Remembers and saves information for future use
- Provides a fixed reference point for later review
- Provides a history
- Allows outsiders to familiarize themselves with situation
- Shows evidence of the analysis process used
- Encourages equal participation in a group

Helpful Techniques for Documentation

Check any you plan to use:

- ☐ Tape butcher paper sheets on walls or windows and keep notes on them.
- ☐ Record what is said and decided on flip charts.
- ☐ Use brief statements and short words that convey the meaning.
- ☐ Have the team itself draft documents, rotating the chore.
- ☐ Tape record brainstorming meetings and have them transcribed.
- ☐ Have a stenographer present to take notes.

EVALUATE YOUR TEAM MEETING

The next time you're in a team meeting, try this experiment to bring focus to the individual roles. After the meeting, have each team member answer the questions on the *Team Problem-Solving Questionnaire.* Then discuss each participant's reactions with the group. The objective is to discover how communication works best in this setting. Either you will find that each team member has naturally gravitated toward adopting a specific role, or you need to define your team meeting responsibilities better.

TEAM PROBLEM-SOLVING QUESTIONNAIRE

1. How was the agenda chosen?
2. Who led the discussion? Why?
3. Did you publicly record issues presented? How?
4. Did all team members participate? If no, why not?
5. Was a consensus reached? If no, why not?

THE BOTTOM LINE

Next time you are part of a problem-solving or decision-making meeting complete the following form to help you zero in on the points that were well-handled and those that could be improved.

MEETING EVALUATION FORM

CRITERIA	0 to 10 RATING (10 = High)

Preparation

• Participants informed ahead of time. _____

• Participants fully prepared for their role and contribution. _____

• Participants committed to dealing with common issues. _____

• Comfortable, uninterrupted set-up room. _____

• Started on time. _____

• Clear, well-presented agenda. _____

Organization

• Agenda followed efficiently with flexibility. _____

• Focused on one issue at a time. _____

• All viewpoints of each issue fully considered before moving on. _____

• Smooth dialogue occurred through coordinated interchange of speaking and listening roles. _____

• Good pace maintained reflecting team momentum. _____

30

CRITERIA	0 to 10 RATING (10 = High)

Participation

- Participants actively contributed to a balanced interchange. _____
- Participants clearly presented their ideas and sincere feelings. _____
- Participants listened attentively to others' contributions. _____
- Participants responded directly and constructively to others' input. _____
- Spontaneous combustion of creative energy and thought stimulated full disclosure of ideas. _____

Climate

- Spirit and emotional level of group was high. _____
- Discussion dealt with issues and their solution, not personalities and their conflicts. _____
- Individuals accepted others' viewpoints without personal attack or nonverbal put-downs. _____
- Members supported the moderator and recorder as they guided the group. _____
- Disruptions and interruptions were handled smoothly. _____

Closure

- Final judgments suspended until all input tapped. _____
- Succinct summaries recapped progress and acknowledged results. _____
- Discussion steered effectively to consensus and then stopped. _____
- Action items clearly announced and documented. _____
- Follow-up monitoring mechanism established. _____
- Meeting ended on positive feeling and mutual understanding. _____

SIX STEPS TO
TEAM PROBLEM SOLVING

The next six parts of this book cover a systematic method of team problem solving and decision making. Following is a list of the steps you will cover:

STEP 1: RECOGNIZING THE PROBLEM

STEP 2: LABELING THE PROBLEM

STEP 3: ANALYZING THE CAUSE OF THE PROBLEM

STEP 4: EXPLORING OPTIONAL SOLUTIONS TO THE PROBLEM

STEP 5: MAKING A DECISION TO SOLVE THE PROBLEM

STEP 6: CREATING AND FOLLOWING AN ACTION PLAN
TO IMPLEMENT THE SOLUTION

PART IV

STEP 1:
PROBLEM RECOGNITION

STEP 1: PROBLEM RECOGNITION

Problem solving and decision making begins by recognizing that a situation needs a resolution. Sometimes a problem gradually builds without being noticed until it surprises you. Even when the trouble is obvious, it is a good idea to start with Step 1.

Problem Recognition examines the "tip of the iceberg."

THE ICEBERG OR 80/20 RULE

No matter how large the tip of an iceberg seems, 80 percent of it lies below the surface of the water.

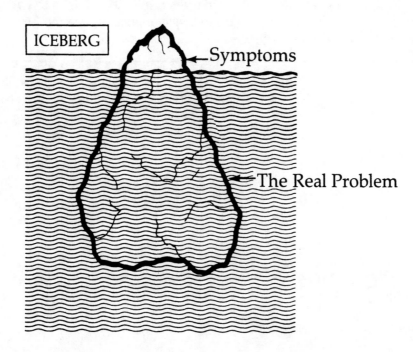

It is the same way with problems. No matter how serious or stressful the first encounter with a problem may seem, it is only a symptom of the underlying trouble or real problem.

Symptoms may be trivial, like one minor defect, or they may be serious issues that must be dealt with quickly, such as falling production levels. Regardless, they are simply side effects of the real problem that lies beneath the surface.

The Iceberg Rule reminds you to have patience. You've got to understand the whole problem before rushing off to solve it. So examining, researching, investigating, tabulating and studying are the watchwords of Step 1.

INVOLVING STAKEHOLDERS

Before you start digging into your iceberg, make sure all the right people are involved. Problems often seem to affect others in unexpected ways and you can't assume that your team members have all the data that you need to solve the problem. A common problem recognition activity is to identify, get input and possibly involve other stakeholders.

A stakeholder is anyone with a stake in the outcome of a project, affected directly or indirectly by a problem or with approval/veto power over decisions.

Effective problem solving ensures that all necessary stakeholder viewpoints are considered or represented during discussions. The best insurance to finding the right solution and guaranteeing buy-in to its implementation is to widen the view of a problem at the beginning. To do this systematically, use the following Viewpoint Selection Worksheet.

Stakeholder Viewpoint	Who Can Best Represent Them?	What Is Their Primary Motivation?	How Should You Involve Them?

OPENING DISCUSSION—
A GOOD PLACE TO START

Problem recognition often starts with a discussion to gather perceived symptoms from those involved. An iceberg may look different when viewed from different angles. Open-minded listening and genuine empathy are required to objectively assess other viewpoints. The objective is to get as much related information as possible "on the table."

During an opening discussion, impressions of the problem may change. What may seem like a technical problem may turn out to be a personality conflict between programmers who don't share information with each other. Studying the human factors (soft symptoms) involved is important to really understand the problem. These include: feelings, divergent opinions, frustrations, personal reactions and hearsay. These are not hard scientific data (hard symptoms), but valuable nonetheless. During the opening discussion, you should discover all of the problem's effects and consequences, both hard and soft symptoms and uncover all initial viewpoints of the situation.

Once viewpoints are listed, it's helpful to categorize them as **hard** or **soft.**

Hard Data	**Soft Data**
Facts, results, events, history, statistics, forces, goals, procedures, physical phenomena, observable deviations, time factors, trends, productivity, quality and performance levels.	Feelings, opinions, human factors, frictions, attitudes, satisfaction levels, stresses, frustrations, personality conflicts, behaviors, hearsay, intuition, "gut" reactions, mental blocks.

HOW MUCH IS TOO MUCH?

How far do you take Problem Recognition? You could say that getting all the facts (hard) and feelings (soft) is your target. The trouble is to know when you've discovered them all. Actually, you will continue collecting facts and uncovering impressions throughout all the steps of the PS/DM process.

Here's a general guideline: You've completed Step 1 when everyone agrees that a problem needs resolution, and when all initial perceptions have been heard, listed and categorized.

PROBLEM RECOGNITION TOOLS

There are five tools in Step 1 that will help you recognize a problem:

> **1. Symptom Identification**
>
> **2. Problem Containments**
>
> **3. Research Methods**
>
> **4. Data Collection Interviews**
>
> **5. Team Brainstorming**

Each tool will be examined individually:

1. Symptom Identification: The *Symptom/Fact List* is a simple form used to tabulate all visible manifestations, consequences and effects. It is compiled by discussing and listing the initial data and perceptions of everyone involved.

Following is an example of a Symptom List filled in with some of the facts from the Consumer Tech Case Problem on page 12.

Symptom/Fact	Hard	Soft
Current product selling well	✔	
New product promises dramatic new improvements	✔	
Engineering wants to make change now		✔
Production department has component problems	✔	
Poor quality likely based on test results	✔	
Marketing Manager ready to announce new product		✔
Finance Manager worried because inventory levels high	✔	✔
Meetings lead nowhere		✔
Heated arguments		✔

Search for both hard and soft data. They're not always distributed 50-50, but you must examine both sides.

TEAM CASE PROBLEM: PROBLEM RECOGNITION

It is time to begin working through the situation you selected on page 4, directly using the PS/DM Outline steps. So before going any further, document everything you know, think and feel about your Team Case Problem on the following worksheet.

SYMPTOM/FACT LIST

Symptom/Fact	Hard	Soft

PROBLEM RECOGNITION TOOLS (continued)

2. Problem Containment: Problem containment means taking quick, temporary action to treat the symptoms of a problem and keep them from getting worse by using a quick-fix, band-aid or patch. Problem containment is designed to protect the team's customer, limit the damage, localize the problem, prevent it from spreading and buy time while the team solves the problem. Here are some quick problem containment tools:

- Rapidly investigate where threats to survival are coming from.
- Brainstorm immediate responses to "stop the bleeding" by localizing the problem.
- Creatively consider adapting past solutions for cheap short-term action on the new symptoms.
- Apply trial and error by flailing around until something works to relieve the current stress.

Dangerous consequences can occur when underlying problem symptoms aren't addressed. The worst impact is that a band-aid may be perceived as a final, permanent solution. When the immediate stress is relieved, attention may be shifted to other fires. Reliance on containment creates a repeating cycle which produces helpless and hopeless feelings. In a sense, problem containment is a type of addiction which only gets worse until root causes are found and addressed.

EXAMPLE

You have a team member with a morale problem. Friends try to cheer the person up with little success. You send the person to human resources for counseling with some temporary improvement. You go back to human resources several times for more help with little result. Later you find the teammate's son gets into lots of fights at school and the personal situation is the source of the morale problem.

GROUND RULES

- Do the minimum problem containment.
- Make containment actions quick, expedient and inexpensive.
- Prominently label all symptomatic solutions as temporary stop-gaps.
- Learn from containment actions to better understand the underlying problem and extend what works to the long-term.
- Aggressively continue the PS/DM outline steps.

3. Research Methods: The *Data Collection Process* will help you systematically study the background and effects of the problem. This ten-step process leads you through designing and conducting an investigation of the problem. The *Data Collection Worksheet* on the facing page includes a series of methods you may choose for your study. A sheet outlining **Sample Target Data** is shown on page 43.

DATA COLLECTION PROCESS

- Identify the overall kind of information needed in order to define the problem. (Use the *Data Collection Worksheet*).

- Select the data collection methods best suited for this type of information.

- Define the specific target data you hope to collect with each appropriate technique (See *Sample Target Data*).

- Collect the data required.

- Analyze the data for patterns.

- Establish a method to confirm the analysis, such as an experiment or more focused data collection process.

- Collect data to confirm the pattern.

- Document data and analysis in understandable form.

- Prepare a visually-oriented presentation if others need to use your analysis.

- Present your data and analysis.

DATA COLLECTION WORKSHEET

To be successful, first identify what target data you're after, and then design your research to focus in that direction.

General Information Needed To Define The Problem	
Data Collection Method	**Specific Target Data**
Survey Questionnaires	
One-on-One Interviews	
Production Statistics	
Quality Statistics	
Financial Statistics	
Work Sampling	
Technical Experiments	
Time/Motion Studies	
Checksheets	
Focus Groups	
Other	

SAMPLE TARGET DATA

Results
Production levels   _____
Quality levels   _____
Error and rework levels   _____
Customer satisfaction   _____
Performance against target   _____
Expenditures versus budget   _____
Profit margin   _____
Return on investment   _____

Resources
Personnel and training   _____
Time   _____
Capital   _____
Production capacity   _____
Physical space   _____
Equipment   _____
Inventory   _____

Organization
Structure and function   _____
Roles and responsibilities   _____
Personnel policies and procedures   _____
Management performance   _____
Strategic planning system   _____
Organizational communication system   _____
Management information reporting system   _____
Management style and corporate culture   _____
Staff morale   _____

External Environment
Other departments   _____
Vendors   _____
Labor   _____
Economy/industry   _____
New technology   _____
Marketplace   _____
Job market   _____
Educational institutions   _____
Political   _____
Competitors   _____
Public goodwill   _____

Obligations
Stockholders   _____
Contractual agreements   _____
Legal restrictions   _____
Labor contracts and laws   _____
Government regulation   _____
Environmental considerations   _____
Social responsibility   _____
Financial commitments   _____
Employee health and welfare   _____

PROBLEM RECOGNITION TOOLS (continued)

4. Data Collection Interviews: Typically the team that starts the PS/DM Outline in motion doesn't have all of the relevant data. The research process can become extensive. Many problem-solving and decision-making teams assign team members to conduct one-on-one interviews or group meetings as an initial data-gathering tool.

Data collection interviews are results-oriented discussions specifically designed to understand an individual's view of the problem. The interviewer poses questions, listens and takes notes, but does not talk much. It is critical to know what needs to be asked before the interview.

The checklist on the next page suggests some appropriate queries. This list can be used as a data collection planning aid. When trying to discover a problem that someone hasn't been completely up front about or dealing with a team that doesn't really understand the situation, check off those questions that you think will get you the information you need.

One word of caution: Interviews can be inefficient or unproductive unless carefully structured in advance. Individual meetings are time consuming and voluminous notes take time to analyze. However, face-to-face meetings generate the most reliable information so they need to be seriously considered.

DATA COLLECTION INTERVIEW

QUESTIONS TO UNCOVER PROBLEMS

Check those you plan to use to study your case problem:

☐ How are things going?
☐ What problems have you had lately?
☐ You seem troubled/upset/worried lately. What's happening?
☐ What do you feel has been different around here lately?
☐ What do you think changed?
☐ How has your work been going?
☐ Where do you need help?
☐ What are you satisfied or dissatisfied about?
☐ What do you find confusing?
☐ What is your position on this matter?
☐ What's on your mind?
☐ Lately I've noticed some indications of lateness/slower work/lower quality. What do you think?
☐ You don't seem to be yourself these days. How come?
☐ What are your feelings about this (conflict/situation)?
☐ What opinions do you have about this problem?
☐ What (tensions/problems/disagreements/misunderstandings/conflicts/troubles) have you been aware of lately?
☐ What is your evaluation of this situation?
☐ Do you think we've been seeing eye to eye lately?
☐ Where do you think our views differ?
☐ What have I done that you (disagree with/object to/dislike/disapprove of/not understand/are confused about)?
☐ What about your viewpoint/attitude do you feel I've missed?
☐ What do you think are our chances of success on this program?
☐ What ideas and suggestions do you have regarding this project?
☐ In what areas do you feel confident/a lack of confidence?
☐ What's bugging you?
☐ What's happening?
☐ What's wrong?
☐ Who is involved and how?
☐ How do you see what's going on?
☐ How does the problem impact you?

PROBLEM RECOGNITION TOOLS (continued)

5. Team Brainstorming: Brainstorming is typically a creative discussion where people build on each other's contributions to produce a comprehensive picture of the situation. Like the interview format, planning is required to make it work. Brainstorming must be led and managed effectively to keep the conversation focused.

Brainstorming with all team members may be sufficient for problem recognition if the group has enough data. If not, you may want to consider adding stakeholders.

The question "What do we know about this problem?" (or possibly others from the list *Questions To Uncover Problems*) provides the right focal point for group brainstorming as a data collection tool. Done right, you can help create tremendous creative leaps through joint energy.

AN UNPRODUCTIVE BRAINSTORMING SESSION

BRAINSTORMING GUIDELINES

Following are some helpful guidelines to apply to your brainstorming sessions. The discussion moderator's role takes on added importance if this method is to be successful. If team members edit, judge, react negatively or just frown at another's contributions, brainstorming breaks down.

Question: The discussion moderator clearly announces the focus of the session—the key question the team will be answering.

Post: The recorder writes down this key question.

Toss Out: All participants toss out as many ideas as possible.

Accept: All ideas, however impractical or crazy, are accepted.

Record: The recorder posts all ideas for everyone to see.

Prompt: The discussion moderator keeps posing the key question without variation to keep the process on track.

No Editing: The discussion moderator reminds the participants, as necessary, that no one is allowed to edit, criticize or evaluate any suggestion overtly or covertly until the process is done.

Build: Participants build on others' ideas. This triggers new thoughts which snowball the team process.

Synergy: By focusing this interaction, the team taps the creative energy of each participant and fuses it in a chain reaction—This is synergy, a combined or cooperative action which is more productive than the sum total of all individual efforts.

BRAINSTORMING GUIDELINES (continued)

Use the Brainstorming Guidelines and evaluate your success with the following list.

Guideline	Yes/No
• Was the question clearly presented and posted for all to see?	_____
• Were participants drawn out by noticing their body language and attitudes?	_____
• Were participants questioned and coaxed only as needed?	_____
• Was all input acknowledged?	_____
• Was everyone encouraged to participate equally?	_____
• Did the recorder write down all new contributions?	_____
• Did the team help the recorder capture key ideas accurately?	_____
• Did the process stay on track?	_____
• Were ideas constructively built on previous contributions?	_____
• Were new points of view proposed if the creative flow lagged?	_____
• Did the discussion moderator and recorder remain neutral without evaluating or steering the discussion to their own views?	_____
• Were the ground rules of brainstorming reinforced by immediately policing any editing, criticism or evaluation?	_____
• Did the team stay stimulated and energized?	_____
• Was any consensus recognized and summed up when it occurred?	_____

PROBLEM RECOGNITION QUIZ

Before you move on to Step 2 in the PS/DM Outline, answer the following items true or false to determine if you have satisfactorily completed Problem Recognition.

True/False

Everything you know about the problem has been documented, including all facts and symptoms.

_____

A wide circle of viewpoints involved in or affected by the problem were represented in your problem recognition discussions.

_____

Customer perceptions and supplier input have been included.

_____

All parties feel their viewpoints and perceptions have been included and their voices heard.

_____

Your initial investigations balanced the focus on different types of facts, i.e. both hard and soft data.

_____

All assumptions were considered while studying the problem and then verified or discarded so that the situation was approached openly and objectively.

_____

Any pent-up emotions were vented to clear the air and get to the real issues on everyone's mind.

_____

Questions, information gaps or assumptions about the problem were thoroughly researched using fact-finding techniques and the data collected was added to your symptom/fact list on page 39.

_____

You haven't studied the problem to death, but did only enough initial discussion and data collection to be able to analyze the key trends and issues.

_____

Everyone involved recognizes that there is an issue needing to be resolved.

_____

PART V

STEP 2:
PROBLEM LABELING

STEP 2: PROBLEM LABELING

After completing Step 1, you should have a wealth of data on your problem. Even so, it may be confusing and you still may not know what kind of a problem you have. Team members may have different interpretations of the same issue.

After a problem recognition session on our Consumer Tech example, some labeled it a manufacturing problem. Others called it a marketing problem. Still others felt it was a petty personality conflict. A management analyst looking from the outside would label it a planning problem. Each reaction has some validity.

A problem will look different from different vantage points. Those doing the looking may label it with different words even though they're talking about the same issue. Whether differences of opinions are about details or major issues, disagreement blocks the necessary teamwork to resolve things.

THE ICEBERG RULE AGAIN

This difference of viewpoint can be called *The Lifeboat Corollary* of the Iceberg Rule. (A corollary is a secondary rule derived from a major principle.)

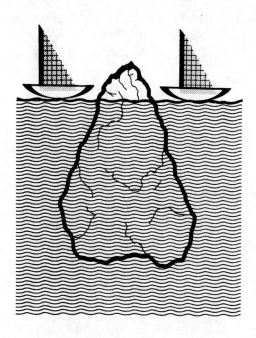

People in each lifeboat view the obstacle that sunk their ocean liner from a different angle. *The Lifeboat Corollary* states that when this occurs it is not possible to agree on descriptions. A common example is a manager who says an employee has a negative attitude. Does the employee buy that? Not usually. In fact, the result is usually that the worker feels the boss is the one with a distorted outlook.

WHAT IS A PROBLEM LABEL?

Step 2 attempts to identify and label all sides of the conflict in a way that everyone can accept. The label can be a phrase that highlights the key issue or the major obstacle. It should describe how things are affected, what needs to change and the scope of the problem.

For example, everyone in the Consumer Tech situation would agree there was: *Disagreement on how to proceed with the new product feature. One group wanted to introduce the new feature now and the other wanted a more methodical implementation plan.*

The result of Problem Labeling is a simple agreed-upon statement of the common denominators of the problem. You need to identify the central issue that needs resolution to define a unifying statement of the main problem.

WHY BOTHER?

Why go to the trouble of generating a label? A label functions as a **clearcut reference point** to focus on during the solution and decision-making process.

The label is like the flag shown below that every lifeboat can see from any direction. The dotted arrow indicates that the function of the label is to lead to the hidden reaches of the iceberg (or problem to be solved).

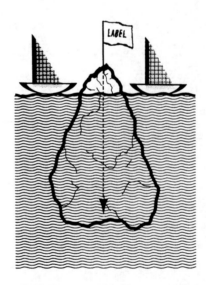

More importantly, all viewpoints must agree on what is to be solved. Outward dissension or internal disagreement at this point will destroy any chance for the logical analysis in Step 3. If those involved can answer *"Yes, that's the problem"* to a label, then they own their part of the problem. They'll be involved from the inside and really want to help solve the problem.

HOW TO FIND A PROBLEM LABEL

There are four tools that will help you find a label for a problem:

1. **Data Analysis**
2. **Brainstorming**
3. **Force Field Analysis**
4. **Key Word Analysis**

Let's take a closer look at each:

1. Data Analysis: The most straightforward way to find a workable label is to sift through the symptoms identified earlier to locate a common denominator. The *Data Analysis Worksheet* helps you think this through. Here's how you use it:

Fill in key **symptoms** in the left column. Search for patterns. Examine symptoms to identify recurring factors. Categorize symptoms in related groups to identify the **type** of problem at hand. Examples of types are: technical, work habits, interpersonal, organizational, personnel, hardware, political, schedule, financial, service, efficiency, communication, etc. Look for common **denominators** until the central issue is clear.

DATA ANALYSIS WORKSHEET

Symptoms	Type	Denominators
Common Denominators/Patterns:		

HOW TO FIND A PROBLEM LABEL
(continued)

2. Brainstorming: Use a *Problem Label Worksheet* to list possible statements of the problem. One popular question used in brainstorming is: *"How are things different from the way we want them to be?"* Other possible target questions are:

- *"What is the problem?"*

- *"What is the central issue?"*

- *"How does the existing situation differ from the ideal scene?"*

- *"What do we want to cure or eliminate?"*

- *"What type of problem are we involved in?"*

- *"What conflict of ideas or intentions are we involved in?"*

Be sure you define all sides of the conflict. One way to accomplish this is to define what specific situation you would like to change and what the obstacle is to this change. *"Record breaking temperatures during August"* isn't a problem until you add *"are killing our garden."* If the second side of the problem was *"are killing elderly citizens who can't afford air conditioning,"* you can see how a label would shift the focus.

The *Sample Labels* on page 58 gives actual examples of labels developed in Problem-Solving workshops.

WORKSHEETS AHEAD

PROBLEM LABEL WORKSHEET

DIRECTIONS:

Develop possible statements of the problem below by defining all sides of the conflict. First brainstorm central issues and then discuss goals. Then identify which are the key answers to each question. Then combine the key answers into problem statements until you find one that everyone can agree on.

What are the central issues of this problem?

What goals are blocked by these obstacles?

What statements that incorporate the key answer to each question above, best describes the problem?

SAMPLE LABELS

We can't meet the fixed inflexible customer ship date for documentation of new software due to continuing engineering changes right up to the last minute.

Lack of communication at shift turnover prevents the next shift from knowing how to handle unresolved problems quickly.

A new software program doesn't meet the specifications and can't be fixed in time to meet the announced one-month release date.

We need to work with a teammate, but we can't stand each other.

An accounting program is needed for regular timely invoices, but no matter what's done to fix it, the program keeps crashing.

The team keeps getting more work assignments than can be handled at once in a quality way, but all of them are assigned ''number one priority'' with a due date of ''as soon as possible.''

We need to fix a customer's problem on the phone but he/she is too emotional to give the facts.

A Label Worksheet is provided on the facing page for your use.

LABEL WORKSHEET

HOW TO FIND A PROBLEM LABEL
(continued)

3. Force-Field Analysis: A two-column Force-Field Analysis process helps to identify a label for a problem. Two suggested applications are presented, an *A versus B* format and an *Obstacles* format.

The *A versus B* format generates a label which defines two conflicting forces. For example,

> *"We should introduce the new product feature right away versus we should proceed carefully until we handle manufacturing and inventory concerns."*

The *Obstacles* format lets you list what you want or what you need and then what prevents you from getting it. For example,

> *"We want to introduce the new product feature right away, but quality problems prevent this from being a great idea."*

FORCE-FIELD ANALYSIS:
A Versus B

What do you want?	What don't you want?

FORCE-FIELD ANALYSIS:
Obstacles

How do you want things to be? What do you need?	What obstacles prevent you from getting it?

4. Key Word Analysis: Key Word Analysis is a method of defining pivotal or disputed words or concepts. Because communication is critical to effective problem solving and decision making, semantics sometimes becomes a barrier. Semantic problems occur when different people have different meanings for the same
key words. Using the *Key Word Analysis Worksheet* on the next page will clarify disputed words and terms to help come up with clearer and more acceptable labels.

To conduct a Key Word Analysis:

1) Select the word/term that seems to be the hang-up.
2) Write it in the top box of the worksheet.
3) Have the team define this key word specifically in as many ways as possible.
4) Select one meaning everyone agrees on and include that definition in your label, or replace the offending word in your original label with a more acceptable word.

In the Consumer Tech case, *quality* is an interesting word to define. Here are the initial definitions from members of the team.

SAMPLE KEY-WORD ANALYSIS WORKSHEET

Keyword Quality	
Definition	
Engineering Manager ⟶	Acceptable rejects (usually 5% or less)
Quality Manager ⟶	Zero defects
Marketing Manager ⟶	"Best" on the market
Finance Manager ⟶	Product with the highest profit margin
President ⟶	Product which makes the stock price soar

Key-Word Analysis is only a supporting technique that provides problem solvers and decision makers with a valuable troubleshooting tool.

KEY-WORD
ANALYSIS WORKSHEET

Key Word

Define the key word as specifically as possible in as many ways as you can:

TEST YOUR WORK

Regardless of which method you use to arrive at a label, it's a good idea to test its effectiveness before proceeding. The *Problem Label Quiz* summarizes what makes an effective label. Run down the list, evaluate your proposed label and adjust it accordingly. Experience has shown that inadequate labeling is one of the biggest reasons for poor problem definition.

PROBLEM LABEL QUIZ

Does the label...	Yes	No
Specify what **aspect** of what problem you want to solve?	☐	☐
Explain what you want to change with a **short** and simple statement?	☐	☐
Identify **all sides** of the conflict or what the obstacle is to the stated goal?	☐	☐
Appear **self-explanatory** and clear to outsiders?	☐	☐
Specifically document the **key issue** without generalities?	☐	☐
State what you want to cure **without** dictating the solution?	☐	☐
Define how wide a **scope** you want to address without being too vague or too narrow?	☐	☐
Generate **agreement** from all sides of the conflict?	☐	☐
Identify the **ownership** of the problem (who HAS it)?	☐	☐
Provide the focus to **steer** your analysis in the right direction?	☐	☐

TEAM CASE PROBLEM: PROBLEM LABEL

Apply Step 2 of the PS/DM Outline to your Team Case Problem by following these directions...

- Analyze your Symptom List (page 39) to identify what you all feel are common denominators or patterns.

- If the central issues of the problem aren't yet clear, use one of the Force-Field Analysis worksheets (pages 61 or 62) to narrow your team's focus.

- Fill in any conclusions on the Problem Label Worksheet (page 57) and brainstorm to answer the questions completely.

- Combine phrases from your list into a short problem statement that is acceptable to everyone.

- If you reach an impasse, use Key Word Analysis (page 63) to get unstuck and finalize a consensus problem label.

- Check that your label meets the requirements of Step 2 using the Problem Label Test on the next page.

PART VI

STEP 3:
PROBLEM ANALYSIS

STEP 3:
THE PROBLEM-CAUSE ANALYSIS

Problem-Cause Analysis produces the true problem definition. So why have we taken valuable time with Steps 1 and 2? Because it is extremely difficult to sort through the mental and emotional issues that cloud a problem. Previous steps helped create general awareness of what the problem is and isn't. Now we will sort out the **causes,** contributing forces or stimuli, that raised the problem in the first place, from the **effects**, symptoms and by-products of the causes.

Step 3 looks for the root cause of the problem. The root cause is a controllable, solvable force which explains why the problem exists. Chester Barnard, an early author on the process of management, called this "the limiting factor." As chief executive of a large regional telephone company several decades ago, he found that the only problems which reached his desk were ones with a missing link. When he was able to ferret out this missing link or "limiting factor," a problem could finally be resolved once and for all.

THAT ICEBERG AGAIN

A dentist once pointed out that the term **root cause** doesn't fit the image of *The Iceberg Rule.* Well, maybe so, but the picture still demonstrates that we're searching for the basic core of the iceberg.

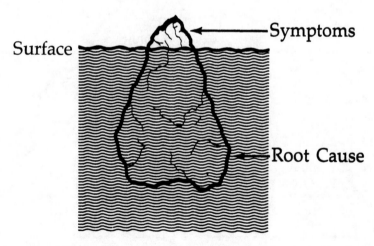

During Step 3, you will identify contributing forces that make the problem worse, sort through partial explanations that are possible causes, and weed out the by-product effects. You may think you've found the answer but the roots are still undiscovered. As you analyze your answers, the layers beneath the surface show that often partial explanations are found for why the problem exists. The **root cause** is at the bottom. It's the pivotal reason that started the problem in the first place and must be dealt with in order to find a long-term workable solution.

A SPECIFIC EXAMPLE

The layers beneath the surface of the iceberg illustrate a significant feature of the anatomy of problems. Typically, people try to fix the superficial symptoms instead of the root cause.

FOR EXAMPLE: a worker hears a rumor from an inside source about plant closings and assumes the worst—*"I'm going to lose my job."* Even though the rumor isn't true, it creates insecurity, so the worker puts out feelers for a new job. A supervisor hears about it and starts giving the "cold shoulder" treatment to the seemingly disloyal employee. If job offers fall through, the worker is now stuck with bad working conditions.

The employee may not understand this compounding sequence or be able to communicate with the supervisor about the foolish assumption that was made. Or, the worker may feel the need to protect an inside source.

The layers look like this, with the latest symptoms on top and the more fundamental causes below:

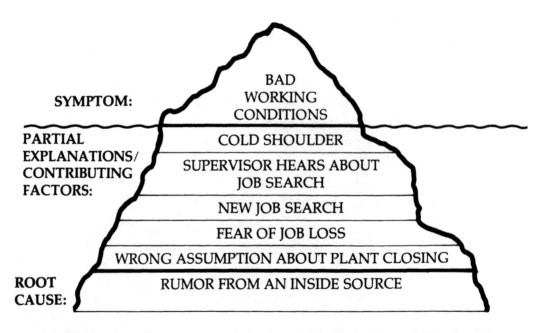

If this snowballing series of events were openly examined it could be cleared up. A little temporary embarrassment might remain but no permanent damage would be done.

YOU CAN HANDLE IT

Sometimes Problem-Cause Analysis yields a root cause that seems unsolvable. This factor can't be the actual root cause because it's not a controllable force that can be dealt with.

Some years ago an insurance branch office ran into severe cash problems early in the spring. The causes were traced back to a snowstorm at the corporate headquarters some weeks earlier. During the extreme winter weather, no one could get to work and the mail stopped for several days.

Was the weather the root cause? Absolutely not. It was a partial explanation, but why would bad weather, not uncommon at that time of year, suddenly cripple the branch? The Problem-Cause Analysis showed cash wasn't managed properly to prepare for this worst case scenario that winter. The root cause was because the branch controller was recuperating from surgery without a replacement. Until someone took the financial reins (and maybe a new policy prevented unfilled key employee positions in the future), more financial problems would result.

REMOVE THE KEY

The root cause explains why a problem persists, reappears and repeatedly draws people into stress, frustration and confusion. It's like a keystone—the one brick that holds the arch together.

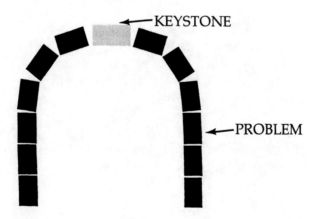

Find the keystone, remove it with a good solution and the problem will collapse.

When those involved have an uplifting *"Aha!"* experience that fully explains the situation, you've found the root cause. "Aha" is a term for the moment of recognition and realization. Often the keystone of a problem is right under your nose, but you didn't notice how important that particular factor was.

THE CONSUMER TECH ROOT CAUSE

When Consumer Tech's management team analyzed their *disagreement on how to proceed with the new product,* they found many contributing factors. Ultimately it was traced to the Board of Directors and some overly-optimistic preliminary reports about the successful test results of the new toothbrush. The Board was wildly excited about the potential effect on the stock price if the product would hit the market ahead of the competition.

This explained the source of the underlying pressure to introduce the new toothbrush immediately. But the Board didn't have the whole story. Several quality and inventory issues remained unresolved. So the root cause was defined as:

> *An incomplete briefing of the Board regarding the Electronic Toothbrush.*

How did this happen? Some enthusiastic staff members passed initial glowing reports to the Board. This is no crime in an open shop. It is natural to want to spread good news to higher ups. No one is to blame for the root cause. That's not the point. The purpose of Problem-Cause Analysis is to learn what happened so successful corrective action can be taken.

Note how different this root cause is from unilateral pressures to resolve the problem. These forces contributed to why the problem existed and partially explained why it persisted. But they weren't enough. That's the power of the root cause. You find a missing explanation that everyone can get behind and you finally have a chance for a lasting fix.

Unfortunately just handling the root cause—giving the Board the whole story now—won't solve the entire problem. But until they have been briefed completely, no problem resolution is likely.

/

DISTINGUISHING CAUSE FROM EFFECT

During Step 3 you analyze the data you have collected or need to research. Then you look for cause/effect relationships until you find the most fundamental underlying cause. You keep turning over stones and looking underneath until there's nothing left to discover.

Sometimes distinguishing cause from effect is tricky. The dictionary defines a cause as **"anything which produces an effect"** and an effect as **"that which is produced by a cause."** Big help, right? It helps to think of **causes** as forces that create or worsen problem symptoms, and **effects** as the consequences resulting from causes. But when you're lost between the top and bottom of an iceberg, cause and effect can be confusing.

Try out the *Cause-Effect Analysis Exercise* on the facing page to assess and sharpen your skills. This situation analyzes the dilemma of a computer programmer in the Engineering Department of Consumer Tech who is leading the development of a new application. The lead programmer refused to accept the results of the code review. This is a meeting in which a program is gone over with a fine tooth comb to see if it will do what's intended. Can you tell cause from effect?

EXERCISE AHEAD

74

CAUSE-EFFECT
ANALYSIS EXERCISE

LABEL: Lead programmer disagrees with results of recent code review.

DIRECTIONS: Classify the following factors as either CAUSE (C) or EFFECT (E). Check the answers at the bottom of the page to see if you labeled the factors correctly.

Factor	Cause (C) or Effect (E)
1. Heated words recently between programmers.	_____
2. Different programming methods used prior to review.	_____
3. Programmer frustrated since new programming methods introduced.	_____
4. No training in new methods.	_____
5. Lack of supervision by lead programmer.	_____
6. Name calling during code review.	_____
7. Lead programmer given "do it your own way" authority.	_____
8. Old database design selected.	_____
9. 280 hours to fix bugs found in code review.	_____
10. No one enjoys working with lead programmer.	_____
11. Extra staff added as result of poor progress.	_____
12. Lead programmer displayed "know-it-all" attitude.	_____
13. Little user input considered in design of new code.	_____

TEAM CASE PROBLEM:
CAUSE ANALYSIS

By this point in our PS/DM Outline, you have identified quite a few causes. If you've documented Steps 1 and 2 for your *Team Case Problem* thoroughly, you can review the facts, symptoms, proposed labels and key word definitions, searching for contributing forces. Transfer the causes you've already identified to the following worksheet. This can be a major time saver, but requires the ability to tell causes from effects. If you can't distinguish between cause and effect, you'll end up transferring too many items.

Problem Label
Possible Causes
Root Cause

SIX TOOLS TO IDENTIFY PROBLEM CAUSES

Problem-Cause Analysis is probably the most demanding action of the entire PS/DM outline.

There are six tools that will help you identify causes:

1. **Brainstorming**
2. **Positive/Negative Forces Analysis**
3. **Charting Unknowns**
4. **Chronological Analysis**
5. **Repetitive Why Analysis**
6. **Cause/Effect Diagram**

1. Brainstorming: You can add to your list of potential root causes with brainstorming. Possible questions to use as your focal point are:

"What caused the problem?"
"Why does the problem exist?"
"Where did it start and where did it come from?"
"Why doesn't it resolve itself?"
"What caused it in the first place?"
"What changed right before things got messed up?"
"Why do we keep getting sucked back into the situation?"
"Why won't things improve no matter what?"

2. Positive/Negative Forces Analysis: The now familiar two-column worksheet, *Positive/Negative Forces Analysis For Causes*, can be used to stimulate thinking to add to the list of causes. By going back and forth from what minimizes the trouble to what makes it worse, new contributing forces come up that didn't occur to anyone before.

POSITIVE/NEGATIVE FORCES ANALYSIS FOR CAUSES

What forces lessen or minimize the problem?	What forces worsen or contribute to the problem?

(Use the above headings to create your own worksheet.)

3. Charting Unknowns: Sometimes problem-solving and decision-making teams run dry before they really look comprehensively at the issue. To break through these blind spots, use the *Charting Unknowns Worksheet* to energize creative thinking. In a sense, this is just another brainstorming question but applied with reverse psychology. Mental blocks may develop from focusing too hard on what you do know about the problem. By asking *"What don't we know about the problem?"* hidden facts emerge or new research directions are suggested.

CHARTING UNKNOWNS WORKSHEET

Statement of the problem
What is not known about the problem?

4. Chronological Analysis: The layered drawing of the iceberg on page 70 shows how unsolved problems evolve. A bad decision causes a production problem. A band-aid solution works temporarily but creates side-effects. Quick fixes are found for these by-products but they don't stick. Months later no one remembers where it all started.

Using the *Chronological Problem Analysis,* it is possible to recall the sequence of events leading up to the snarled-up situation. Starting from present time, list the major symptoms or causes and examine when each started. This type of investigation reveals cause-effect relationships by identifying what happened before the last blowup. Often you find that an intermediate problem was actually caused by an inappropriate solution made earlier.

CHRONOLOGICAL PROBLEM ANALYSIS WORKSHEET

Major symptom/cause	When did it start?	What happened then?

(Use the above headings to create your own worksheet.)

SIX TOOLS TO IDENTIFY
PROBLEM CAUSES (continued)

Using the *Chronological Problem Analysis Worksheet,* the causes from the Consumer Tech programmer's disagreement were listed in chronological order with the most recent cause at the top.

- Lack of supervision of programming team.
- Lead selected old database design.
- Different programming methods used prior to review.
- Little user input considered in design of new code.
- No training on new methods.
- Lead programmer given "do it your own way" authority.
- Lead programmer displayed a "know-it-all" attitude.

In this particular case it was determined that the lead programmer's attitude was a personality trait that wasn't about to change. The final analysis showed that giving a "know-it-all" *Do It Your Own Way* authority was what really precipitated the continuing troubles. This is not to point the finger in blame. Some decisions look like the most expedient solution at the time, but later breed other trouble. Hindsight is the best teacher, so put your emphasis on **what**, not **who**.

It helps to plot the results of this analysis on a *Problem Timeline.* This sample gives you an idea of how such a chart looks when done. The clear picture may not answer any specific questions itself, but it shows what to ignore and exactly where to look when you're searching for the root cause.

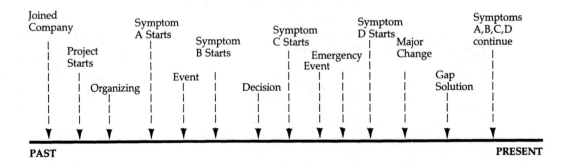

PROBLEM TIMELINE

PAST   PRESENT

5. Repetitive Analysis: Extensive analysis sometimes generates many potential causes but no clear *"Aha!"* regarding the root. It helps to trace the evolution of the problem with a **Repetitive Analysis.** This procedure distinguishes between the most fundamental causes and their intermediate effects. The logic process used strongly resembles the idea of uncovering a piece of paper which hides another piece of paper, hiding another, etc.

If the root cause doesn't appear during your initial search, find one underlying factor that seems to be most fundamental. Write it in the first box of the *Repetitive Why Worksheet.* Then ask *"What caused that?"* or *"Why is that a problem?"* repetitively until you locate the basic problem on the chain. An example follows to show how this works.

REPETITIVE WHY WORKSHEET

```
┌─────────────────────────────────────────────────────────┐
│                                                         │
│                                                         │
│                                                         │
└─────────────────────────────────────────────────────────┘
```

Which was caused by...

```
┌─────────────────────────────────────────────────────────┐
│                                                         │
│                                                         │
│                                                         │
└─────────────────────────────────────────────────────────┘
```

Which was caused by...

```
┌─────────────────────────────────────────────────────────┐
│                                                         │
│                                                         │
│                                                         │
└─────────────────────────────────────────────────────────┘
```

Which was caused by...

```
┌─────────────────────────────────────────────────────────┐
│                                                         │
│                                                         │
│                                                         │
└─────────────────────────────────────────────────────────┘
```

Which was caused by...

```
┌─────────────────────────────────────────────────────────┐
│                                                         │
│                                                         │
│                                                         │
└─────────────────────────────────────────────────────────┘
```

SIX TOOLS TO IDENTIFY
PROBLEM CAUSES (continued)

REPETITIVE WHY WORKSHEET—SAMPLE

Problem: *Irate customer on the phone*

Fifth time put on hold

Which was caused by . . .

Inability to get automatic toothbrush to work as designed

Which was caused by . . .

Incorrect written instructions about product

Which was caused by . . .

Wrong instruction manual in box with new product

Which was caused by . . .

Vacation replacement packers didn't have written policy to follow and inserted wrong manual in product package.

6. Cause/Effect Diagram: Another way to logically think about Problem-Cause Analysis is to create a *Cause/Effect Diagram.* This is often called a fishbone diagram because its lines resemble that of a discarded skeleton after a good fish dinner. The diagram visually categorizes forces into related groups for simpler analysis.

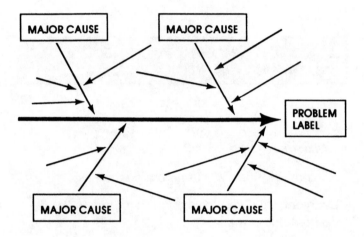

Here is what Cause/Effect Diagram would look like for Engineering change errors:

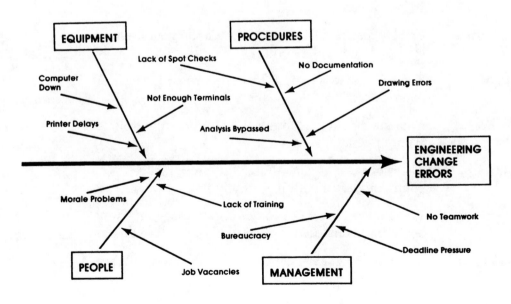

HAVE YOU DONE IT?

Don't move to the solution phase until you are sure you have found the root cause. Test your tentative conclusion using the following checklist *How to Know When You've Found the Root Cause* for verification. To ensure you've analyzed a problem fully and correctly, check the proposed root cause against questions on the checklist. It must pass *all* of the tests to be the true root cause. If the results of these evaluations aren't conclusive, continue working until the tests are passed. The second phase of the PS/DM Outline will break down without the right root cause.

HOW TO KNOW WHEN YOU'VE FOUND THE ROOT CAUSE OF A PROBLEM

	Test Questions	Yes/No
Dead End:	You ran into a dead end when asking, *"What caused the proposed root cause?"*	_____
Conversation:	All conversation has come to a positive end.	_____
Feels Good:	Everyone involved feels good, is motivated and uplifted emotionally.	_____
Agreement:	All agree it is the root cause that keeps the problem from resolving.	_____
Explains:	It fully explains why the problem exists from all points of view.	_____
Beginnings:	The earliest beginnings of the situation have been explored and understood.	_____
Logical:	The root cause is logical, makes sense and dispels all confusion.	_____
Specific:	Your statement gets to the exact point of the trouble without generalizations.	_____
Control:	The root cause is something you can influence, control and deal with realistically.	_____
Hope:	Finding the root cause has returned hope that something constructive can be done about the situation.	_____
Workable:	Suddenly workable solutions, that deal with all the symptoms begin to appear.	_____
Stable:	A stable, long-term, once-and-for-all resolution of the situation now appears feasible.	_____

WHEN SHOULD YOU DO WHAT?

Step 3 is the most demanding and confusing step in the PS/DM process. More options are presented here than anywhere else in the PS/DM Outline. This wealth of tools sometimes overwhelms problem-solving and decision-making teams. The *Root-Cause Analysis Program* is a general sequence of techniques which serves as a starting point agenda.

Adjust the order of steps to best approach your team's situation.

ROOT-CAUSE ANALYSIS PROGRAM CHECKLIST

Date
Completed

Process: Agree on which process the team will use at each point in the analysis. _____

Roles: Select an appropriate discussion moderator and recorder. _____

Brainstorm: Brainstorm an appropriate question, then document all answers on a simple form such as the **Cause Analysis Worksheet** on page 75. _____

+ / − Forces: Use a *Positive/Negative Forces Analysis* to add to your list of possible causes. _____

Evaluate: Evaluate which cause is most fundamental and underlying all others. _____

Diagram: Group or categorize the possible causes and determine which category is most basic, using a *Cause/Effect Diagram.* _____

Repetitive Analysis: Use the *Repetitive Worksheet* to trace the most basic cause down to its root. If you hit a dead end, try another starting point down a different path. _____

Others: Use other techniques to add to or evaluate the possible causes on your list until you determine the root cause. _____

Test: When you think you've got it, test your hypothesis using the checklist *How To Know When You've Found the Root Cause of a Problem.* _____

Persevere: If your first hypothesis doesn't prove out, go back and continue your analysis until you succeed. It will be a frustrating waste of time if you skip to solving the problem without an ''*Aha!*'' experience at this point. _____

PART VII

STEP 4:
OPTIONAL SOLUTIONS

HOW NOT TO CONSIDER
OPTIONAL SOLUTIONS

STEP 4:
OPTIONAL SOLUTIONS

Finally work can begin on the second phase of the PS/DM Outline, decision-making. Deciding on a workable solution for the root cause begins with Step 4. This is not a lengthy or complicated step, but is vital in generating agreement on the ultimate decision.

Step 4 is called "Optional Solutions" because the goal is to complete a list of conceivable alternatives. You're looking for any strategies which will address the root cause and resolve the problem once and for all. A complete list of alternatives is essential before proceeding to Step 5.

WHY AS LONG A LIST AS POSSIBLE?

Insisting on a comprehensive list prevents you from rushing off impulsively with the first idea that sounds good. There's a chance that if you follow the first off-the-cuff proposal, it will be inferior, inadequate or unbalanced. You've come this far by avoiding short-cuts. Don't give in to the temptation now.

Draw on the creative powers of those involved to examine all possible courses of action. This will ensure all viewpoints are considered. Though this may not be enough to preclude differences of opinion during decision-making, it at least creates the respect and acceptance so often missing in conflict situations. Everyone may have his or her own hidden agenda and/or pet solution. So be sure to get these in the open and on the list.

Once you get agreement that every course of action is on the list and will be considered, a team will feel some direct ownership in the decision-making process. And this may help to put the team in the mood of generating consensus later.

An Approach to Creativity

A good approach is to follow the Creativity Flowchart on the next page. The PS/DM Outline is set-up to adhere to this scheme. Brainstorming complete lists certainly encourages this process.

CREATIVITY FLOWCHART

Here's a brief outline of how the creative process works to get teams thinking.

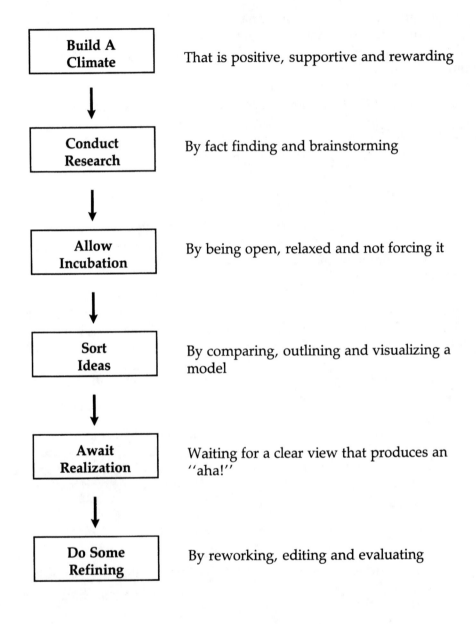

| Build A Climate | That is positive, supportive and rewarding |

| Conduct Research | By fact finding and brainstorming |

| Allow Incubation | By being open, relaxed and not forcing it |

| Sort Ideas | By comparing, outlining and visualizing a model |

| Await Realization | Waiting for a clear view that produces an ''aha!'' |

| Do Some Refining | By reworking, editing and evaluating |

THE CONSUMER TECH CASE PROBLEM UNFOLDS

Consumer Tech came up with the following list of options (in no particular sequence) to solve the problem of their Electronic Toothbrush:

- Let the President make the decision and then get the dissenters in line.

- Fire those who want to introduce the new toothbrush immediately.

- Start a spin-off operation to produce a model with the new feature.

- Fire those who want to go more slowly.

- Threaten to resign to protest pressure from the Board of Directors.

- Schedule a meeting with the Board to make sure they have the necessary information and let them make the final decision.

- Develop a joint planning process involving the Board.

- Let the current thrashing process work itself out...(do nothing).

- Hire a consultant to mediate the process.

Some of the above are more sensible than others. The "replacement" options are downright threatening, but the Consumer Tech management team included them to make the list complete. Once the list is complete, there should be one less thing to argue about, namely: *"Is the best solution on the list?"* If they have done their job, the solution will be on the list.

***BUILD A COMPLETE LIST OF OPTIONS
BY ASKING THE RIGHT QUESTIONS***

OPTIONAL SOLUTIONS (continued)

BUILDING A COMPLETE LIST

There are three tools to generate a complete list of optional solutions:

> **1. Review**
>
> **2. Brainstorming**
>
> **3. Force-Field Analysis**

These tools are designed to identify strategic directions and basic approaches, not specific tasks. To list every helpful action would make the task monumental. Apply a "seeing the forest, not the trees" concept. If you come up with a large number of action tasks instead of strategies, save them for action planning at Step 6.

1. Review: The obvious starting place is to review your notes. The temptation to get rid of symptoms during Problem Analysis is great. You will probably have many possible solutions in your notes from Steps 1, 2 and 3. If so, you have a head start on Step 4. Here is how careful documentation and thorough analysis pays off.

Review any potential solution strategies discovered earlier and transfer them to the *Optional Solutions Worksheet* on the facing page. These may have been ideas on how to resolve the situation, or they may represent actual past attempts to deal with the problem. Since the motto is *"anything goes,"* previous attempts need to be on the list. An earlier flop may work if better focused or old ideas may suggest more workable variations.

Write the root cause you found on page 75 on the following worksheet. Then transfer any solutions that came up during earlier exercises to the bottom.

OPTIONAL SOLUTIONS WORKSHEET

Root cause to solve	
List all strategies that have any chance of working	Evaluation (Step 5)*

*(Leave the Evaluation Column blank until Step 5.)

OPTIONAL SOLUTIONS (continued)

2. Brainstorming: Brainstorming seems to have been made for Step 4. Focus each team member's mind on conceiving any strategies that have the slightest chance of resolving the root cause. Consider incredible proposals, ridiculous or unacceptable approaches, all far-out suggestions and anything pertaining to the resolution of the underlying issue.

Research on meetings shows that conservative teams are much less effective in problem resolution than those willing to consider wild-eyed schemes. Removing blinders and internal barriers may generate some crazy ideas. Typically even harebrained proposals can often be molded into workable paths no one would have dreamed of without unrestrained brainstorming. And that's fun too!

Add to your *Optional Solutions Worksheet* as things progress. Be sure to follow the rules of brainstorming and avoid editing or evaluating until the list is complete. Always include *doing nothing* as one option since this course of action should be consciously considered.

Possible target questions to serve as the focal point for this process are:

"What would solve the problem?"

"What strategy could resolve the root cause?"

"What solutions have already been thought of?"

"What approaches haven't been thought of?"

"How could we stop this situation from recurring?"

"What different methods might work?"

"What crazy ideas might help?"

BRAINSTORMING TOOLS WORKSHEET

Consider using different brainstorming tools for different situations. As your experience grows, consider the pros and cons of each.

Option	Description	Pros	Cons
Card Deck	Each person writes separate ideas on cards or slips of paper which are combined in a deck and discussed by the whole team.		
Round Robin	One person shares an idea with the team verbally, then the next person in order shares an idea, and so on. The discussion continues until everyone has spoken.		
Bouncing Ball	One person catches the ball and volunteers an idea, then throws the ball to another person who volunteers an idea, and so on.		
Popcorn	In any order, individuals spontaneously throw out one-word or short-phrase answers which summarize their position on an issue.		
Free Wheel	All team members spontaneously share ideas at will with the whole team with others building on their ideas.		

OPTIONAL SOLUTIONS (continued)

3. Force-Field Analysis: The *Positive/Negative Analysis For Solutions* can stimulate thinking just as the force-field format did in the past. Since we're looking for solutions, the two columns play **better** against **worse.** This is similar to the worksheet in Step 3 designed to generate causes. New approaches should be added to the master list of optional solutions on page 91.

POSITIVE/NEGATIVE FORCES ANALYSIS
FOR SOLUTIONS

What would make the problem better?	What would make the problem worse?

TEAM CASE PROBLEM: OPTIONAL SOLUTIONS

Continue applying the PS/DM Outline to your Team Case Problem at Step 4 by following these directions...

- Select the appropriate brainstorming tool from page 93.

- Complete your list of solutions by adding to the Optional Strategies Worksheet (page 91).

- Make as complete a flipchart list as possible in the time allowed. Switch questions if you run dry. In other words, don't limit your brainstorming by limited thinking or judgmental discussion. Use Force-Field Analysis (page 94) if necessary. At this point we're just shooting for quantity, not quality, of solutions.

- Number the items on your list for comparison and later evaluation.

PART VIII

STEP 5:
DECISION MAKING

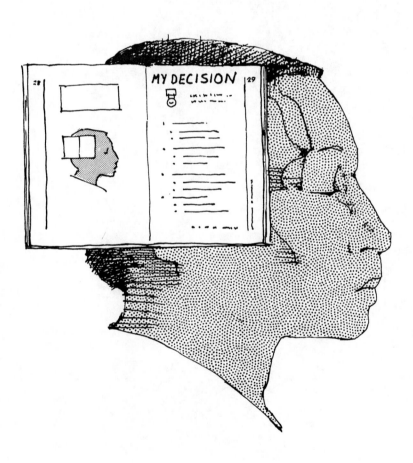

STEP 5: DECISION MAKING

Decision Making is the second half of this book. Yet it's taken us a long time to get here. That's because everything up to this point is designed to make decision making work right.

Step 5 allows you to choose one alternative solution as a course of action. You make a value judgment on what to do about the problem. The result you want is a firm joint decision on the chosen optional solution. This means selecting one strategy from the list in Step 4 that everyone will respect.

Too often decision making consists of abuse of political power, personal preference, poor leadership or a macho demonstration of decisiveness. The PS/DM process is designed to avoid these. Having analyzed the problem thoroughly, determined the underlying root cause and listed possible alternatives the team is able to make an objective, rational, comparative evaluation.

LINE 'EM UP

The philosophy of Step 5 is **evaluation**—This means eliminating the worst choices and weighing remaining options against each other. You will consider ranking, prioritizing and scoring the alternatives to make your choices. The goal is to find the ''right''solution using a practical, scientific process.

By pooling information and considering different viewpoints, teams can usually find better solutions and make better decisions than most individuals. However, this strength can become a weakness. Chances are pretty slim that all team members will think and feel exactly the same way, especially about a controversial issue. If people are left out of a decision-making process, they typically won't support its implementation. Without having their voice heard, there's little chance for emotional ownership, or a sense of buy-in.

You've worked hard to set things up for an objective comparison and you're in a good position to pull it off. Remember that the primary concern is to make a consensus decision. If everyone supports it, it will work and the implementation that you'll design in Step 6 will be carried out.

A Consensus Decision is an idea everyone in the team...

- Sees as a fusion of the information, logic and feelings expressed
- Understands and substantially agrees represents a common reality
- Can live with, go along with, support and accept
- Believes is a workable approach in the best interests of the team

HOW TO MAKE A DECISION

There are eight tools to help the team's decision-making process:

> **DECISION-MAKING TOOLS**
> 1. INFORMAL DISCUSSION
> 2. BRAINSTORMING
> 3. ELIMINATION
> 4. WEIGHING AGAINST GOALS
> 5. WEIGHING AGAINST CONSEQUENCES
> 6. PRIORITIZING
> 7. COMBINATION
> 8. CRITERIA MATRIX

1. Informal Discussion: It is natural to discuss a list of options first. Thinking out loud, bouncing ideas off other people and getting advantages and disadvantages in the open is a healthy starting point for making a decision. You can record any conclusions in the evaluation column of the *Optional Solutions Worksheet* from Step 4. This tool is the least structured process for evaluating options, but it plays a critical role in problem solving and decision making.

2. Brainstorming: Brainstorming wasn't designed for objective decision-making. The momentum of group thinking can sway rational analysis away from a balanced evaluation, but it can be an effective method because of the ideas generated. Possible questions to use as guidelines are:

"How does each alternative solution measure up?"

"Which option seems most workable?"

"Which solution has the best chance to succeed?"

"How risky is each possible solution?"

"Which solution can everyone decide to fully commit to?"

"Which solution do you definitely prefer?"

HOW TO MAKE A DECISION (continued)

3. Elimination: A common occurrence during informal discussion or brainstorming is to discover that some options won't cut it. Eliminating unworkable choices can reduce a long list to something more manageable. You can delete items using specific disqualifying factors such as: cost, risk or time. The following tools may be difficult with an unwieldy list.

Put an "X" next to the options you would eliminate from the list Consumer Tech generated. Then check the answers with those in the upside down box below to see which options Consumer Tech eliminated.

1. Let the President decide and get the dissenters in line   _____
2. Replace those who want to introduce the hands-free option now   _____
3. Start a spin-off to produce a model with the new feature   _____
4. Fire those who want to go slowly   _____
5. Threaten to quit in protest of Board pressure   _____
6. Fully brief the Board and let them decide   _____
7. Develop a joint planning process involving the Board   _____
8. Let the current thrashing process work itself out (do nothing)   _____
9. Hire a consultant to mediate the process   _____

ANSWERS: During the decision-making process, Consumer Tech quickly ruled #2, #4 and #5 as clearly undesirable.

4. Weighing Against Goals: Review your list of remaining options and weigh them against the goals of the organization, department or team performance plan. For this to be successful, an accurate, up-to-date strategic plan is required. Problem-solving and decision-making teams often find it necessary to develop or refine organizational or personal goals at this point.

A useful approach to this tool is to develop a statement of an ideal situation. How you would want things to be if you had total control over circumstances? Then evaluate your alternative solutions against this scenario.

HOW TO MAKE A DECISION (continued)

5. Weighing Against Consequences: You can weigh the potential ramifications of each option using the *Consequences Worksheet* below. List optional solutions in the left column and then predict the likely consequences in the columns to the right. By comparing the contents of one column against the next, you create a risk/reward and cost/benefit analysis. In the *conclusions* column, decide whether the possible benefits and rewards justify the potential costs and risks.

CONSEQUENCES WORKSHEET

Optional Solution	Potential Costs	Potential Risks	Possible Benefits	Possible Rewards	Conclusions

6. Prioritizing: The *Prioritizing Methods Checklist* on the facing page offers six approaches to selecting the best solution from a list. Each method has strengths. Determine which method you think will work best and apply it to your list of options.

You may not be familiar with the second method, *"bubble-up/bubble-down."* It functions like a computer sorting device. In a forced-pair comparison, you take the first two items on the list and decide which is better. If the second wins, it moves to the top of the list. Otherwise leave them as is and move to the next distinct pair. As an example let's use the remaining items in the Consumer Tech list.

1. Let the President decide and get the dissenters in line
3. Start a spin-off to produce a model with the new feature
6. Fully brief the Board and let them decide
7. Develop a joint planning process involving the Board
8. Let the current thrashing process work itself out (do nothing)
9. Hire a consultant to mediate the process

#1 and #3 seem to be in the right order, so leave them as is. When we compare #3 and #6, the "spin-off" option seems less desirable and should move down.

1. Let the President decide and get the dissenters in line
6. Fully brief the Board and let them decide
3. Start a spin-off to produce a model with the new feature
7. Develop a joint planning process involving the Board
8. Let the current thrashing process work itself out (do nothing)
9. Hire a consultant to mediate the process

This process should continue first downward and then upward for all items on the list. A forced-pair prioritizing comparison is finished when there is agreement on the relative position of every item on the list in relation to every other item.

Do you agree with the final order below from the Consumer Tech case or would you organize them differently?

7. Develop a joint planning process involving the Board
6. Fully brief the Board and let them decide
9. Hire a consultant to mediate the process
1. Let the President decide and get the dissenters in line
3. Start a spin-off to produce a model with the new feature
8. Let the current thrashing process work itself out (do nothing)

PRIORITIZING METHODS CHECKLIST

1. Ranking in order of:

      Best ☐

      Most workable ☐

      Reliability ☐

      Most tested and proven ☐

      Least risky ☐

      Staff ability to make it work ☐

      Chance for success ☐

2. Use forced-pair comparison to *"bubble-up/bubble-down"* items resulting in a prioritized list.

3. Get individuals in a group to rate each item and then tabulate ratings using a scale such as:

      5 = Top Preference

      4 = High Preference

      3 = OK

      2 = Maybe

      1 = Slim Chance

      0 = No Way

4. Vote where majority rules.

5. Prioritize by gut feel, intuition or comfort zone.

6. Compromise.

7. Combination: At some point during evaluation, problem-solving and decision-making teams may find that two or more items on the list do not conflict. Solutions that complement each other could work well together. A useful decision-making tool is to categorize remaining options. By combining solutions within a category, it is possible to shorten the list for your final choice. Pool creative thinking on each alternative within a category for more workable outcomes. Decision making then boils down to a more simple job of comparing categories.

The top three options on the Consumer Tech list aren't mutually exclusive. In fact, all have benefits. After some consideration, the management team decided to combine items #7, #6 and #9. Their list now reads like this:

7/6/9. Hire a consultant mediator, fully brief the Board and develop a joint planning process with the Board.

    1. Let the President decide and get the dissenters in line.

    3. Start a spin-off to produce a model with the new feature.

    8. Let the current thrashing process work itself out. . .(do nothing).

SIMPLIFIED DECISION-MAKING

JUST DO IT!

HOW TO MAKE A DECISION (continued)

8. Criteria Matrix: A helpful method to visualize decision choices is a *Criteria Matrix.* This is a chart with alternative solutions listed in the left column, the criteria to measure them across the top and ratings against criteria in intersecting boxes. Summary ratings are calculated by adding the boxes.

To use the Criteria Matrix, you first must develop a thoughtful *Standards and Criteria List.* Criteria are accepted standards, common sense benchmarks or proven yardsticks that indicate what an effective solution would look like. List measurement indicators that tell whether a proposed solution is good, bad or marginal.

You may wish to consider what organizational goals, departmental objectives, and job targets are impacted by the problem. Do validated quality or quantity standards exist? Take into account any time, cost, material or human constraints that need to be considered. What negative consequences should your choice avoid at all costs? Look for benchmarks against which to judge the workability of the items on your list of alternative solutions.

STANDARDS AND CRITERIA LIST

Consumer Tech's Management group developed the following list of criteria.

By what standards and criteria should you judge your optional strategies?

- Effect on stock price
- Expansion of market
- Cost-effectiveness
- Effect on management and staff morale
- Level of risk

The alternative solutions are listed in the left-hand column of the matrix with the criteria listed across the top. It is important to use a key word or phrase. If you use lengthy statements or numbers, the matrix won't visually communicate what you're evaluating.

You can rate options using a **+, −, ?** scale, an **A,B,C** label or a numeric scale of **1 to 3** or **1 to 10.** When using the numeric scale, add up each row to generate a numeric score for each alternative. A weighted evaluation can also be used to give a different multiplier to scores under each criteria. With or without weighting the final ranking comes from adding the ratings in each row. The matrix is helpful in compartmentalizing a complex analysis, but the answer is no more accurate than the individual scores. Other methods of rating may be more appropriate in specific cases. Be sure to define your scale in the box at the top of the matrix before you begin.

CRITERIA MATRIX

Rating scale:

Alternative Solutions	Evaluation Criteria					Summary Rating

In the resulting boxes, you rate each option against each criteria. We'll see how Consumer Tech rated their alternative solutions on the following pages.

HOW TO MAKE A DECISION (continued)

Consumer Tech chose a 5 point scale. Based on your knowledge of the case, rate the options and add up the scores as you see it. Then compare your ratings with those of Consumer Tech which appear on the following page.

CONSUMER TECH CRITERIA MATRIX

Rating scale:
1 to 5, with 5 = best

Alternative Solutions	Evaluation Criteria					Summary Rating
	STOCK	MARKET	COST	MORALE	RISK	
7/6/9. Consultant mediator/Board briefing/joint planning process						
1. President decides and gets dissenters in line						
3. Start a spin-off to produce a model with the new feature						
8. Let the current thrashing process work itself out... (do nothing)						

TEAM CASE PROBLEM: DECISION MAKING

Continue applying the PS/DM Outline to your Team Case Problem at Step 5 by following these directions...

- Use appropriate tools (1, 2 or 3) to concentrate on narrowing your complete list of optional solutions from the exercise on page 95.

- Use appropriate tools (such as 4 and 5) to help the team develop a common sense of which options will work better.

- Decide on the best optional strategy on your narrowed list of solutions using a prioritizing tool (6) or criteria matrix (8).

- If you decide there's more than one necessary or workable solution, organize your top priorities into a combined strategy (7).

- When you've reached a consensus decision, test your proposal with the *Decision Quiz* that follows on page 111.

THE CONSUMER TECH RANKING

Here's how Consumer Tech scored their remaining options:

Alternative Solutions	Evaluation Criteria					Summary Rating
	S T O C K	M A R K E T	C O S T	M O R A L E	R I S K	
7/6/9. Consultant mediator/Board briefing/joint planning process	5	5	4	5	5	24
1. President decides and gets dissenters in line	2	3	5	3	3	16
3. Start a spin-off to produce a model with the new feature	4	5	1	4	1	15
8. Let the current thrashing process work itself out (do nothing)	1	3	5	1	1	11

In this case, the bubble-up/bubble-down process yielded the same result as a Criteria Matrix. This is a good double check. In real life you probably wouldn't apply every decision-making tool. Some will be more appropriate than others. Use your judgment.

The final score for each alternative is only as reliable as the accuracy of each individual rating. This process only breaks down a complex evaluation into a series of smaller judgments. So if the top scores are close, don't make your final decision solely by the results of matrix.

BEFORE MOVING ON

Evaluate your final choice with a *Decision Quiz.* This is done by designing questions to test the workability of your key solution. When evaluating a decision, the form below will determine whether you've picked the ideal decision, the most likely to succeed decision, or the most workable decision. The ideal decision will pass all tests, but may not be workable. In decision making, perfection is secondary to workability.

DECISION QUIZ

Quiz Question	**Yes/No/?**
1. Does it solve the problem and the root cause?	_____
2. Will it realistically accomplish the objectives?	_____
3. Does it satisfy all established criteria?	_____
4. Does it satisfy all people involved and affected?	_____
5. Can workable action plans be developed to implement it?	_____
6. Is there time to implement it?	_____
7. Do the personnel and resources exist to make it work?	_____
8. Will its implementation end the recurrence of the problem?	_____
9. Have all its risks, disadvantages and possible consequences been considered?	_____
10. Is it the best choice in terms of:	
a. Benefits	_____
b. Costs	_____
c. Risks	_____
d. Commitment	_____
e. Workability	_____

PART IX

STEP 6:
IMPLEMENTATION

*AVOID A "DATA DUMP" WHEN
DESCRIBING YOUR ACTION PLAN*

STEP 6: IMPLEMENTATION

The best solution ever conceived and agreed upon won't solve a problem if it isn't put into action. Step 6 concentrates on four phases:

   I. Generating Action Plans to implement the solution decided upon

   II. Considering Contingency Plans if your best plan doesn't work right

   III. Managing the Project you've created to ensure it works

   IV. Standardizing Solutions processes and operations to prevent the problem from ever recurring

I. ACTION PLANNING

An action plan creates a practical program to translate the decision or overall target into reality. A critical result of Step 6 is a complete step-by-step road map of how to implement the decision. An action plan details who will do what, by when. It organizes tasks which implement the decision in the real world. Timing, personnel and other resources must be considered and choreographed into action. Setting performance standards, production and quality targets, plus a follow-up monitoring mechanism is vital to ensure that the plan is carried through.

IS IT WORTH THE TROUBLE?

New teams often ask, *"Why bother to plan at all?"* The answer is simple: You will be much better prepared to adapt and respond even when things go wrong with a plan. The benefits are included in *The Value of Action Planning Checklist* on the next page.

THE VALUE OF ACTION PLANNING

Check those items which would help you implement decisions and solutions.

AGREE

Realistic Actions: They translate decisions into workable realistic actions the team can identify with. ☐

Concrete Programs: They nail down abstract ideas into concrete programs which are achievable. ☐

Specific Assignments: They give specific assignments so individuals know what to do and when. ☐

Clear Expectations: They create clear expectations so the team know how they will be evaluated. ☐

Effective Delegation: They divide responsibility for effective delegation in a simple way. ☐

Mutual Commitment: They build agreement by establishing mutual commitment to the plan. ☐

Coordinate Action: They coordinate action and thus contribute to team-building and teamwork. ☐

Effective Follow-Up: They provide an effective follow-up mechanism by mapping future checkpoints. ☐

Objective Measurement: They establish a basis for objective results measurement. ☐

Clearcut Accountability: They contribute to clearcut accountability by identifying who is responsible for what. ☐

Save Time: They save time by coordinating action and translating decisions into assignments. ☐

Support Workers: They guide team leaders to know how to support workers without over-supervising. ☐

Employee Involvement: They provide good opportunity for employee involvement in the planning process itself. ☐

Ensure Results: They ensure results by focusing all resources in the best possible way. ☐

CONSUMER TECH ACTION PLAN

Here's what an initial sketch of the Consumer Tech action plan looked like. Turn the page to begin creating your own action plan.

Solution: Fully brief the Board, develop a joint planning process and use a consultant to mediate the process					
Action	**Resonsible Person**				
1. Identify outside consultant	President				
2. Investigate problems in manufacturing	Mfg Mgr				
3. Estimate when quality will become reliable	Qual Mgr				
4. Predict how long current inventory will last	Finance Mgr				
5. New feature introduction marketing plan	Marketing Mgr				
6. Brief consultant	President				
7. Fully brief the Board	President				
8. Set up joint planning process	Consultant				
9. Begin joint planning	Consultant				
10. Develop action plan for implementation	President				

SIX ACTION PLANNING TOOLS

There are six action planning tools to help problem solvers and decision makers generate a workable road map to implement their decisions:

1. Review
2. Brainstorming
3. Question and Answer

4. Organize
5. Monitoring
6. Resource Estimation

1. Review: You probably have a number of action terms in your notes from previous steps. After deleting those focused on other root causes or decision stratagies, transfer any workable ideas on to the *Action Item Worksheet*.

ACTION ITEM WORKSHEET

2. Brainstorming: Continue your creative thinking by brainstorming on the *Action Item Worksheet*. Questions which will serve as your target are:

"What needs to be done to make this solution work?"

"How do we get from here to there?"

"Who should do what?"

"What is the most efficient budget and schedule?"

"How will we know if we're on or off track?"

"How will we follow up to ensure completion?"

3. Question and Answer: Use the *Action Planning Question Checklist* to add to your list. Go through the questions one by one and when you feel each has been thoroughly answered, check it off and move on to the next one. This comprehensive approach will help ensure that all bases are covered.

ACTION PLANNING QUESTION CHECKLIST

What is the overall objective and ideal situation? ☐

What is needed in order to get here from there? ☐

What actions need to be done? ☐

Who will be responsible for each action? ☐

How long will each step take and when should it be done? ☐

What is the best sequence of actions? ☐

How can we be sure that earlier steps will be done in time for later steps which depend on them? ☐

What training is required to ensure that all team members have sufficient know-how to execute each step in the plan? ☐

What standards do we want to set for performance? ☐

What level of volume or quality is desirable? ☐

What resources are needed and how will we get them? ☐

How will we measure results? ☐

How will we follow up each step and who will do it? ☐

What checkpoints and milestones should be established? ☐

What are the make/break vital steps and how can we ensure that they succeed? ☐

What could go wrong and how will we get around it? ☐

Who will this plan affect and how can we involve them? ☐

How can the plan be adjusted without jeopardizing its results to ensure the best response and impact? ☐

How will we communicate the plan to ensure support? ☐

What response to change and other human factors are anticipated and how will they be overcome? ☐

SIX ACTION PLANNING TOOLS (continued)

4. Organize: Use the *Action Plan Form* to put all your proposed actions together in an orderly fashion. The *Overall Solution* box should first be filled in with the solution strategy you're trying to implement (chosen in Step 5.) Then, arrange the specific tasks from the *Action Item Worksheet* in sequence in the *Action* column. Next, consider the team members available and assign who will be responsible for what on the form. Individual training and development is too often forgotten in Step 6. Be sure to include who needs to learn what to make the plan work. Now, define what level of volume or quality must be achieved in the *Performance Standard* column.

ACTION PLAN FORM

Date:

Overall Solution:

Action	Responsible Person	Performance Standard	Monitoring Technique	Completion Deadline	Resources Needed
1.					
2.					
3.					
4.					
5.					
6.					
7.					
8.					
9.					
10.					
11.					
12.					
13.					
14.					

5. Monitoring: The next column to complete on the *Action Plan Form* is for *Monitoring Technique*. When you establish a performance standard, you determine how well each function must be done.

However, things never go exactly as planned. You need to establish a communication and follow-up system so that all team members involved stay informed and keep the project on track.

The *Monitoring Techniques Checklist* suggests methods which can be used for each action item. Select the most appropriate, accurate, easiest and reliable method which will show both team and performer how well things are progressing. The best monitoring is self-administered, while the team is watching.

MONITORING TECHNIQUES

☐ Production count statistics
☐ Quality control spot checks
☐ Work sampling
☐ Personal inspection of all work
☐ MBWA (management by walking around)
☐ Checkpoints on action plan
☐ Reflective indicator statistics (measuring indirect consequences)
☐ Trend analysis (typically using graphs)
☐ Compliance reports
☐ Regular activity reports
☐ Tickler file

☐ One-on-one review meetings
☐ Team meetings
☐ Climate/attitude surveys and written questionnaires
☐ Customer/user interviews
☐ Checklist evaluation/audit
☐ Fitness report essay (comparing actual to ideal)
☐ Walk through/role play/dummy run procedure
☐ Budget controls
☐ Grapevine
☐ Gut feel

---

6. Resource Estimation: Timing is another essential element of the monitoring process. Each item needs a firm *Completion Deadline*. Long or complex activities may benefit from one or several intermediate checkpoints as well. Time is a limited and easily expendable resource, especially without careful action planning, though dollars are watched even more closely in well-run businesses. This is the best time to calculate logistics, budgets and other hard resources. Include your estimates in the *Resources Needed* column of the form.

TEAM CASE PROBLEM: ACTION PLANNING

Continue applying the PS/DM Outline to your Team Case Problem at Step 6 by following these directions...

- Start developing a plan to implement the solution you chose in Step 5 by reviewing your earlier work and any action steps already discussed.

- Brainstorm action steps to flesh out your plan. Use the Action Planning Question Checklist (page 119) to ensure you consider everything.

- Sequence and organize the action steps you've listed according to the Action Plan Form (page 120).

- Include Monitoring Techniques from page 121.

- Evaluate the action plan developed using the Action Plan Test on the next page.

ACTION PLAN TEST

After constructing an action plan but before giving the go ahead, evaluate it using the *Action Plan Test.* By testing it against the 14 criteria, you'll get a good sense of its relative effectiveness and completeness. The best action planners religiously play devil's advocate with their draft work, and adjust it wherever necessary until it has the highest chance of coming off without a hitch.

Criteria	Rating
Does your Action Plan identify. . .	**Yes/No**
1. Specific actions	_____
2. Clear responsibilities, targets and standards	_____
3. Realistic deadlines	_____
4. Realistic resource estimates	_____
5. A coordinated sequence of actions	_____
6. Flexibility to change	_____
7. Checkpoints for routine follow-up	_____
8. Reliable control system to measure progress	_____
9. Needed personal development	_____
10. Correctly emphasized priorities	_____
11. Feasible contingency plans	_____
12. Workable agreements for all involved	_____
13. A realistic and workable system	_____
14. A good chance of achieving the ideal scene	_____

II. CONTINGENCY PLANNING

By this time anyone having gone to the trouble of developing an action plan will think it's near perfect. But what about a small dose of humility? Always consider Murphy's Law; *"That which can go wrong, will."* To avoid human and job sacrifices to Murphy's Law, the best insurance is a little contingency planning. Obstacles to successful implementation can be obvious or hidden. Use the *Contingency Planning Worksheet* to help the team think through what could go wrong, what you can do to avoid it and if worst comes to worst, how you will get out of the pickle.

CONTINGENCY PLANNING WORKSHEET

What could go wrong?	How could you prevent it from happening?	How will you fix it if it happens?

One contingency too often ignored is the all-important human factor. People who weren't involved in the PS/DM Outline analysis may misunderstand the solution. Anticipate where you'll run into resistance to change and again decide how to prevent or combat it. The following chart, *How to Handle Resistance to Change*, should provide some helpful suggestions.

HOW TO HANDLE RESISTANCE TO CHANGE

1. Accept It	People need stability and change unstabilizes. Expect resistance, fear and insecurity to the new and unfamiliar.
2. Empathize	Try to understand the reaction by occupying another's point of view for a moment. If you see the personal and emotional impact change creates, you can handle it better.
3. Know Before You Go	Before you introduce change, find out what you're dealing with. Don't rush into the new until you are an expert on the old and current way of doing things. If necessary, wait until an auspicious time.
4. Analyze The Consequences	Who will it affect? How? What might happen that you haven't considered? Consider all possible eventualities and adjust your proposal to maximize the desirable and minimize the undesirable consequences. (If you can't change what you want to, drop it.)
5. Involve Stakeholders	Ask others for input on the new plan, problems it creates, potential benefits, how to best implement it. By asking, discussing, accepting and team problem-solving, not only will stakeholders buy into the change, they'll improve on it and make it more workable.
6. Give Advance Warning	The sooner you announce that change is coming, the better. The longer the lead time, the less the shock and the easier the emotional and intellectual adjustment.
7. Beat The Grapevine	Manage the *PR* (public relations) of your idea effectively. If the idea leaks, and the grapevine precedes your announcement, you've got an extra credibility gap to dig yourself out of.
8. Present It Positively	Sell your idea to everyone affected in a way calculated to appeal broadly, and minimize shock, fear and hostility. Be prepared, composed and constructive—not *spur-of-the-moment* bullheaded.

II. CONTINGENCY PLANNING (continued)

9. Vent Resistance	Sometimes people just need to ventilate the emotional shock of the unexpected and untried without any response from the boss. Letting them blow off steam in a group planning session or even one-on-one first can clear the air for rational thought.
10. Stress Benefits	Initially emphasize the needs and problems of others and how the change will help them, not you. If it's for them, it's more likely to be viewed as desirable and worth the trouble. You can even offer appropriate rewards for swift, smooth cooperation.
11. Explain The Purpose	If people can see why you want to go to all this trouble, maybe they'll join the effort. Ideally, the team will agree, so start your presentation in terms of the organizational problem you want to solve or improvement to accomplish.
12. Reassure Them	An immediate promise from the boss that no one will lose their job, pay or future will help. Anticipate specific individual fears and assure all that the worst won't happen, confidently and realistically.
13. Stress Growth	Many people want to get ahead. Change creates opportunities. If you reinforce new approaches, by highlighting possible chances for advancement and development, you can entice the ambitious ones over to your side.
14. Include Training	In both your plans and announcements, be sure to include enough reeducation and on-the-job training to make the transition smooth. People want to do a quality job, so prevent the fear of failure by promising and conducting supportive training.
15. Change Gradually	Don't expect major readjustment overnight. Plan for step-wise change, fast enough to keep the energy up but slow enough so each step can be smoothly and certainly done.
16. Recognize Your Supporters	Each step of the way acknowledge constructive advice and willing cooperation. A sincere and loud *"thank you"* afterwards will do an awful lot for improving the climate for change next time.

III. HOW TO MANAGE A PROJECT

The following list provides some guidelines to help the team manage the project.

- Chart or graph the project plan for a visible reminder.

- Hold a meeting or event to start the project.

- Issue action items in writing according to the plan.

- Discuss all assignments in conjunction with written action items to ensure understanding and commitment.

- Encourage people, and provide guidance and support as needed.

- Distribute brief synopses of progress and problems to those involved in the project so that everyone stays informed.

- Use Management By Wandering Around so the team won't be surprised.

- Monitor activities routinely and at planned checkpoints.

- Recognize completed steps and check them off the plan.

- Acknowledge individual contributors when they meet their targets.

- Immediately respond to indicators of trouble and act accordingly.

- Adjust the plan as needed to meet the overall project.

- Conduct team meetings when group action is essential to coordinate, adjust or trouble shoot.

- Watch for loose ends as the project winds down and insure they get completed on time.

- Document the entire project, including the plan, midstream changes, learning experiences, problems encountered and solutions that worked.

- Publicly announce successful completion of the project, recognizing all those who contributed.

128

IV. STANDARDIZING SOLUTIONS

To ensure that a problem won't recur, you need to implement standard methods of prevention. Using the tools below, you can standardize the solution and minimize your chances of backsliding.

Here are some the team can choose from to standardize the process or operations that created the problem in the first place.

- Repeat and improve the P.D.C.A. Cycle (plan, do, check, adjust) over and over until procedures work reliably and stably.

- Record past problems and their solutions to learn from them.

- Establish SOP (standard operating procedures).

- Revise and update procedure manuals and documents to reflect any changes in policy to all departments.

- Create a flowchart of standard processes for visual understanding.

- Inform other departments of the problem and solution to ensure widespread understanding.

- Post job aids, placards and posters to remind operators of the SOP.

- Include new material in training programs for future employees' benefit.

- Design a training program specifically for this problem.

- Build a routine monitoring system.

- Encourage workers to monitor themselves.

- Measure quality and results with periodic reviews.

- Transfer problem prevention from inspectors to everyday operators.

- Reinforce new behavior with recognition and rewards.

- Be prepared to respond immediately if the problem recurs.

PART X

SUMMARY

EVALUATION OF OBJECTIVES

After working through the problem-solving and decision-making process presented here, evaluate your team's progress. On a scale of 1 to 10 (10 = high) rate how well you've achieved each of the objectives of this system:

Outline: Understand the systematic rational problem-solving outline. _____

Techniques: Know how to use the various analytical techniques for each phase. _____

Communication: Recognize the vital role communication plays at each step. _____

Questions: Know what questions to ask in order to stimulate communication at each phase. _____

Anatomy: Understand the anatomy of problems and why they persist. _____

Prevent Stress: Understand how to confront problems to prevent future stress. _____

Cause & Effect: Know how to distinguish between problem causes and effects. _____

Label: Know how to label a problem to facilitate discussion and analysis. _____

Root Cause: Know how to find a problem's root cause. _____

Solutions: Know why it's important and how to brainstorm optional solutions. _____

Decisions: Know how to evaluate optional solutions to decide on the most workable strategy. _____

Implementation: Understand the importance of action planning to implement the chosen solution. _____

Application: Know how to use the forms, tools and resource materials to apply the system to real-life problems as they occur in the future. _____

SUMMARY

Answer the following questions to wrap things up and set your sights on the future:

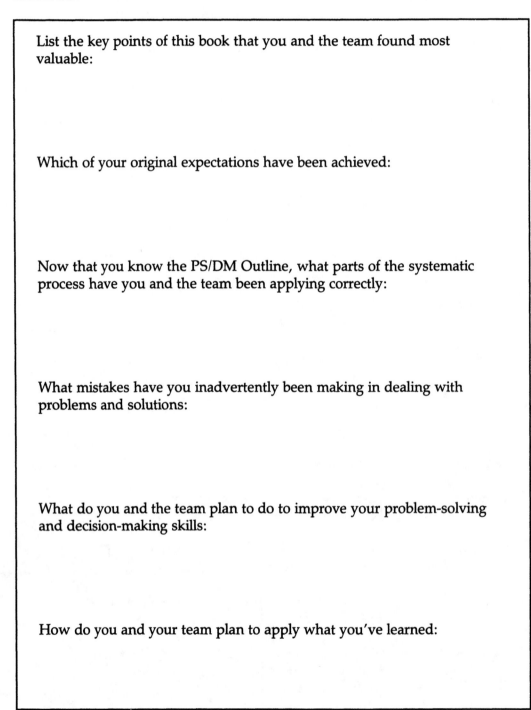

List the key points of this book that you and the team found most valuable:

Which of your original expectations have been achieved:

Now that you know the PS/DM Outline, what parts of the systematic process have you and the team been applying correctly:

What mistakes have you inadvertently been making in dealing with problems and solutions:

What do you and the team plan to do to improve your problem-solving and decision-making skills:

How do you and your team plan to apply what you've learned:

NOTES

NOTES

Also Available

Books•Videos•Computer-Based Training Products

If you enjoyed this book, we have great news for you. There are over 200 books available in the *Crisp Fifty-Minute™ Series*. For more information visit us online at www.axzopress.com

Subject Areas Include:

Management
Human Resources
Communication Skills
Personal Development
Sales/Marketing
Finance
Coaching and Mentoring
Customer Service/Quality
Small Business and Entrepreneurship
Training
Life Planning
Writing